Crocheted Bags, Totes
AND Purses

Crocheted Bags, Totes AND Purses

CROCHET YOUR OWN COLOURFUL AND UNIQUE ACCESSORIES

EMMA FRIEDLANDER-COLLINS

CICO BOOKS

This book is dedicated to Kate Sully, the best friend a girl could ask for.

This edition published in 2025 by CICO Books
First published in 2016 as *35 Crocheted Bags*

10 9 8 7 6 5 4 3 2 1

Text © Emma Friedlander-Collins 2016, 2025
Design, illustration and photography © CICO Books 2016, 2025

A CIP catalogue record for this book is available from the British Library.

ISBN: 978-1-80065-421-1

Printed in China

Editor: Rachel Atkinson
Designer: Geoff Borin
Photographer: Gavin Kingcome
Stylist: Luis Peral
Techniques illustrator: Stephen Dew

Senior designer: Emily Breen
Art director: Sally Powell
Creative director: Leslie Harrington
Head of production: Patricia Harrington
Publishing manager: Penny Craig
Publisher: Cindy Richards

CICO Books
an imprint of Ryland Peters & Small Ltd
20–21 Jockey's Fields, London WC1R 4BW
www.rylandpeters.com
Email: euregulations@rylandpeters.com

The authorised representative in the EEA is Authorised Rep Compliance Ltd., Ground Floor. 71 Lower Baggot Street, Dublin, D01 P593, Ireland
www.arccompliance.com

All instructions in this book contain both metric and standard (imperial) measurements. Please use only one set of measurements as they are not interchangeable.

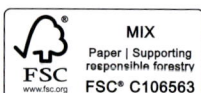

MIX
Paper | Supporting responsible forestry
FSC® C106563
www.fsc.org

Contents

introduction

"Have nothing in your house that you do not know to be useful, or believe to be beautiful." William Morris

I must have first read that quotation when I was about 13 and it has never left me. This collection of crocheted bags grew from a desire to carry things with me that I genuinely love, which bring me joy through their design and also enhance my day by being useful.

When I dash out of the house in the morning, I not only have all my daily 'essentials' to carry, but also those for my two young boys as well. There are wet wipes, juice boxes, snacks, toy cars, Lego, pens, you name it – anything to keep them busy if we end up out for a coffee somewhere! All the bits and pieces were getting thrown into a tote bag that came free with a magazine, simply because I could fit everything in it. Every day this slightly grubby, dreary-looking thing would make me feel a little bit sad, so I grabbed my trusty hook and a ball of yarn and set to work. This book is the result.

Pushing myself and developing new crochet skills all the time has been really exciting, and I learned a whole variety of new techniques to make the projects in these pages. This means there's something for everyone – from adventurous beginners to seasoned crocheters.

I get genuine pleasure out of using these totes, handbags, and cases, and I hope you will too.

Love

Emma xxx

before you begin

Crochet is great for making bags and accessories. A tight stitch creates a strong and versatile fabric for a sturdy tote, whereas open stitches are perfect for market bags and pretty evening bags alike. A finished crochet piece also lends itself to being embellished and accessorized, be it with cross-stitch, appliqué, or a few tassels and pompoms, all of which you will find within the pages of this book. Play to your heart's content and make the piece your own! The following information will set you on course to creating a really professional looking, finished project.

Yarn

Pure cotton and acrylic yarns, along with wool blends, are ideal for crocheted purses as they tend to hold their shape better and do not stretch as easily as 100% wool or silk fibres. However, so long as you take time to line the project to prevent stretching, using wool and silk yarns will give you a beautiful finish. Match the type of yarn to the project – a child's backpack, such as the Chunky Envelope Rucksack (page 21) needs to be tough to cope with the demands placed on it, so a sturdy acrylic will work perfectly and also benefits from being machine washable. The Little Purse (page 100), on the other hand, may be something you make as a treat for yourself or to give to a friend, so using a more luxurious yarn will make it extra special.

Tension

A guide for the tension is given with each pattern, and while matching this exactly is not as paramount when making bags and purses, it is important to achieve a tension as close as possible to the one provided so your finished make has the same look, feel, and size as shown in the photographs. Check your tension before starting the project and make adjustments by switching the size of the hook – if your tension is too tight and the stitches on your swatch are smaller than those recommended, try using a hook one size larger. Similarly, if your stitches are too large, switch to a hook one size smaller and rework the swatch. See page 114 for information on tension swatches.

Stitch patterns

You will find a variety of stitch pattern techniques used throughout the book, ranging from basic double and treble crochet fabrics to more complex lace stitches. A few of the projects in this book use the tapestry technique of carrying a number of yarns at once. As long as it's practical, when you have up to 3 or 4, I'd recommend working over them so they become an integral part of the fabric as seen in the Aztec Shoulder Bag (page 46) or Tassel Tote (page 26). This makes for a nice, sturdy bag with much less stretch and no need for lining. If you find that you have too many yarns or that they are interrupting the colours in projects such as the Candy Skull Bag (page 67) and Foxy Crochet Carry Case (page 96), just work in the yarn not in use every few stitches, carrying them rather than cutting and rejoining, and line the finished project to maintain a neat finish.

Reading charts

A number of patterns, including the Rose Handbag (page 70) and Scout Pocket Bag (page 76) include charts that when followed, enable you to easily create the same colourwork pattern featured in the sample. Each square of the chart represents a stitch and by carefully reading each row or round you will gradually produce the same graphic shown in the photographs. Charts are generally read from bottom to top, and from right to left for right-side rows and left to right for wrong-side rows. When working in the round, the start of each round is on the right-hand side of the chart.

Blocking

Taking time to carefully finish your project will give it a really neat and professional look and crocheted projects really benefit from being blocked once complete. Not only does blocking help the pieces to lie neatly and to the given measurements, it also opens up the stitches to really show off the pretty details of your hard work. You can block your finished make with either steam from the iron, or by soaking in lukewarm water and pinning into shape to dry. Remember to check the ball band of the yarn for specific details on washing the yarn, and take care when steaming acrylic and acrylic blend yarns as they can easily stretch out of shape. Cotton and silk yarns can be blocked firmly to encourage the fibres to sit neatly in place. See page 118 for more information on blocking.

Sewing and stitching

A sewing machine is useful for constructing the bag linings, but it is advisable to hand-sew the linings into the bags themselves. The crocheted fabric and lining material will have different amounts of stretch, and hand sewing enables you to control this more evenly. I generally use polycotton fabrics for lining as they are hardwearing and come in a myriad of different colours and patterns. To measure the lining, I lay the finished purse on the fabric, cut a rough approximation, allowing a little extra for the seam allowance, but it is worth double checking the measurements are correct with a tape measure before cutting the fabric – measure twice, cut once! Take time to tack the lining in position first and then stitch into place to ensure you have the correct fit. Note that the fabric measurements given in the pages do not include seam allowances.

Straps and accessories

The straps used in the samples are more of a guide, as it may be difficult to find exact replicas for many of these pieces. However, these are the finishing touches that will bring your bag to life, so don't be afraid to experiment and find materials that really personalize the bags and express who you are. Old leather belts and recycled straps are ideal, but equally chain, cord, ribbon, bias binding, webbing – all sorts of things – can work really well, so take your finished crochet piece out shopping and try some things on!

Equipment

Crochet hooks: The patterns in this book indicate the size of hook to use with the yarn listed for the project, but you can adjust these where necessary to accommodate yarn substitutions and to achieve the correct tension. How you hold the hook is a matter of preference – left-handed or right-handed, some like to hold their hook in a pencil-grip, while others prefer to hold it in their fist. There is no right or wrong way so long as you are able to move your wrist freely and can comfortably work neat and even stitches. See page 108 in the techniques section for further guidance on holding the hook and yarn.

Crochet hooks used in the book:

UK/Metric	US
2.75mm	C/2
3.25mm	D/3
3.5mm	E/4
4mm	G/6
4.5mm	7
5mm	H/8
6mm	J/10
8mm	L/11
10mm	N/15
12mm	P

Locking stitch markers: These are a great addition to your crochet tool kit and are used to keep track of the beginning of a round when working a spiral in projects such as the Zigzag Glasses Case (page 84). Remember to move the stitch marker up with each round or use two in tandem with one another. Safety pins can be used, but take care they don't snag or leave rust marks on the yarn.

Tapestry and yarn needles: Used to secure the ends of the yarn at the start and end of the project and also where colour changes occur. For heavier weight yarns, try using a split eye needle or a small crochet hook to secure in the ends neatly.

Tape measure: Always handy for checking finished sizes.

Sewing needle and thread: Along with making linings and inserting zips, you will also need a sewing needle and thread for attaching buttons and embellishments to your project.

Rust-proof pins: For holding your project when seaming and in shape whilst blocking.

Skill level

Each project includes a star rating as a skill level guide and you will find the project includes the techniques listed below:

✱ ✱ ✱ Projects suitable for new crocheters using basic stitches with minimal shaping.

✱ ✱ ✱ Projects using basic stitches, repetitive stitch patterns, simple colour changes, and simple shaping and finishing.

✱ ✱ ✱ Projects using a variety of techniques, such as tapestry crochet or lace stitches, with mid-level shaping and finishing.

chapter 1 **totes and holdalls**

This shopper was made to replace a plastic version I'd been using for years. What I especially love about this pattern is the upcycled yarn it is created with – not only is the shopper a really useful size and shape, it's also got great sustainability credentials.

spring shopper

Yarn

Hoooked Zpagetti (super chunky weight; 100% recycled jersey fabric; 120m/131yds per 850g/30oz cone)

1 cone of shade Neon Melon (A)
1 cone of shade Print (B)

Hooks and Notions

10mm (US N/15) crochet hook
Locking stitch marker
Tapestry needle

Tension

8 sts and 8 rows to 10cm (4in) measured over double crochet

Finished Size

43cm (17in) wide x 25cm (10in) deep, measured flat

16.5cm (6½in) handle drop

Abbreviations

See page 125.

Pattern Notes

The shopper is worked in a continuous spiral – use a locking stitch marker to keep track of the start of a round and move it up as you complete each one.

For the Shopper

Using yarn A and 10mm (US N/15) hook, make 15ch.
Round 1: 2dc in second ch from hook (missed ch does not count as st), 1dc in next 12 ch, 3dc in end ch. Working up the other side of the ch, 1dc in next 12 ch, 1dc in end ch, join with a sl st in first dc, place marker for beginning of round. *(30 sts)*
Round 2: 2dc in each of first 2 sts, 1dc in next 12 sts, 2dc in each of next 3 sts, 1dc in next 12 sts, 2dc in last st, do not join and work in a spiral as follows moving the marker up as you complete each round. *(36 sts)*
Round 3: 2dc in each of first 3 sts, 1dc in next 14 sts, 2dc in each of next 4 sts, 1dc in next 14 sts, 2dc in next st. *(44 sts)*
Round 4: 1ch, 1dc in BLO of each st around.
Round 5: 1dc in first st, 2dc in next st, 1dc in next 21 sts, 2dc in next st, 1dc in next 20 sts. *(46 sts)*
Round 6: 1dc in first 2 sts, 2dc in next st, 1dc in next 22 sts, 2dc in next st, 1dc in next 20 sts. *(48 sts)*
Round 7: 1dc in first 2 sts, 2dc in next st, 1dc in next 23 sts, 2dc in next st, 1dc in next 21 sts. *(50 sts)*
Fasten off yarn A and join yarn B.
Round 8: Using yarn B, 1dc in first 3 sts, 2dc in next st, 1dc in next 24 sts, 2dc in next st, 1dc in next 21 sts. *(52 sts)*
Round 9: 1dc in first 4 sts, 2dc in next st, 1dc in next 25 sts, 2dc in next st, 1dc in next 21 sts. *(54 sts)*
Round 10: 1dc in first 5 sts, 2dc in next st, 1dc in next 26 sts, 2dc in next st, 1dc in next 21 sts. *(56 sts)*

Round 11: 1dc in first 6 sts, 2dc in next st, 1dc in next 27 sts, 2dc in next st, 1dc in next 21 sts. *(58 sts)*
Round 12: 1dc in first 7 sts, 2dc in next st, 1dc in next 28 sts, 2dc in next st, 1dc in next 21 sts. *(60 sts)*
Round 13: 1dc in first 8 sts, 2dc in next st, 1dc in next 29 sts, 2dc in next st, 1dc in next 21 sts. *(62 sts)*
Round 14: 1dc in first 9 sts, 2dc in next st, 1dc in next 30 sts, 2dc in next st, 1dc in next 21 sts. *(64 sts)*
Rounds 15–20: 1dc in each st around.
Round 21: 1dc in first 21 sts, make 25ch, miss 11 sts, 1dc in next 21 sts, make 25ch, miss 11 sts. *(2 handles made)*
Round 22: *1dc in first 21 sts, work 27dc around 25ch from previous round; rep from * once more, sl st in first dc to join. Fasten off.

Making Up and Finishing

Weave in all loose ends and gently steam block into shape.

Cut a 2m (2yd) length of yarn A. Using the photographs for guidance, weave the yarn through stitches near the top of the bag, starting and ending in the middle of one side of the bag and leaving two equal lengths of yarn. Tie the yarn into a bow and trim ends.

When I was a little girl and heading to a friend's house for a sleepover, I would take my Grandad's canvas army kit bag. It was the perfect size to pack my pillow and PJs in and reminded me of home. This crochet version is an homage to that bag. It is light enough for my little boys to pack with their teddies and toothbrushes when they now go on sleepovers.

kit bag

Yarn

Katia Big Ribbon (super chunky weight; 50% cotton, 50% polyester, 72m/78yds per 200g/7oz ball)

 2 balls of 08 Khaki (A)
 3 balls of 20 Green (B)

Hooks and Notions

10mm (US N/15) crochet hook

Tapestry needle

104cm (41in) length of 4cm (1½in) wide acrylic webbing

Sewing needle and matching thread

Tension

8 sts and 9 rows to 10cm (4in) measured over double crochet

Finished Size

25cm (10in) diameter x 45cm (17¾in) tall

Abbreviations

See page 125.

For the Bag

Using yarn B and 10mm (US N/15) hook, make a magic ring.

Round 1: Work 1ch (does not count as st throughout), 6dc into the ring, sl st in first dc to join. (6 sts)

Round 2: 1ch, 2dc in each st around, sl st in first dc to join. (12 sts)

Round 3: 1ch, *2dc in next st, 1dc in next st; rep from * around, sl st in first dc to join. (18 sts)

Round 4: 1ch, *2dc in next st, 1dc in next 2 sts; rep from * around, sl st in first dc to join. (24 sts)

Round 5: 1ch, *2dc in next st, 1dc in next 3 sts; rep from * around, sl st in first dc to join. (30 sts)

Round 6: 1ch, *2dc in next st, 1dc in next 4 sts; rep from * around, sl st in first dc to join. (36 sts)

Round 7: 1ch, *2dc in next st, 1dc in next 5 sts; rep from * around, sl st in first dc to join. (42 sts)

Round 8: 1ch, *2dc in next st, 1dc in next 6 sts; rep from * around, sl st in first dc to join. (48 sts)

Round 9: 1ch, *2dc in next st, 1dc in next 7 sts; rep from * around, sl st in first dc to join. (54 sts)

Round 10: 1ch, *2dc in next st, 1dc in next 8 sts; rep from * around, sl st in first dc to join. (60 sts)

Round 11: 1ch, 1dc in BLO of each st around, sl st in first dc to join.

Rounds 12–20: 1ch, 1dc in each st around, sl st in first dc to join.

Rounds 21–43: Change to yarn B. 1ch, 1dc in each st around, sl st in first dc to join.

Round 44 (Drawstring holes): 1ch, *1dc in next 2 sts, 1ch, miss 1 st; rep from * around, sl st in first dc to join.

Round 45: 1ch, *miss 2 sts, 3dc in ch-sp; rep from * to end, sl st in first dc to join.

Round 46: 1ch, 1dc in each st around, sl st in first dc to join. Fasten off.

Making Up and Finishing

Weave in all loose ends and gently steam block into shape.

To make the drawstring: Cut a 1m (40in) length of yarn A. Knot the ends and weave through the holes made in Round 44.

To make the strap: To give a little more structure to the bag, sew the webbing strap across the bottom of the bag. Stitch the top of the strap to the inner edge at the top of the bag.

TIP Add a few more shades into the mix and work in stripes to create a colourful bag.

This is a great pattern for beginners and one of the most useful things I've ever made. I have these in virtually every room in the house: one by the front door for keys and mail, one in my bedroom for beauty products, and there are at least three in my office for hooks, yarn and other crafty materials.

project basket

Skill Level ★ ★ ☆

Yarn

Hooooked Zpagetti (super chunky weight; 100% recycled jersey fabric; 120m/131yds per 850g/30oz cone)

　1 cone of Aqua (A)
　Small quantity of Print (B)

Hooks and Notions

10mm (US N/15) crochet hook

Tapestry needle

Tension

8 sts and 8 rows to 10cm (4in) measured over double crochet

Finished Size

20cm (8in) diameter x 12.5cm (5in) tall

Abbreviations

See page 125.

> **TIP** This basket has so many possibilities for customization – make it deeper by working additional rounds before creating the handles in Round 16, or add extra stripes alternating colours every round after Round 8.

For the Basket

Using yarn A and 10mm (US N/15) hook, make 3ch, sl st in first ch to form a ring.

Round 1: 1ch (does not count as st throughout), 6dc into ring, sl st in first dc to join. *(6 sts)*

Round 2: 1ch, 2dc in each st around, sl st in first dc to join. *(12 sts)*

Round 3: 1ch, *2dc in next st, 1dc in next st; rep from * around, sl st in first dc to join. *(18 sts)*

Round 4: 1ch, *2dc in next st, 1dc in next 2 sts; rep from * around, sl st in first dc to join. *(24 sts)*

Round 5: 1ch, *2dc in next st, 1dc in next 3 sts; rep from * around, sl st in first dc to join. *(30 sts)*

Round 6: 1ch, *2dc in next st, 1dc in next 4 sts; rep from * around, sl st in first dc to join. *(36 sts)*

Round 7: 1ch, *2dc in next st, 1dc in next 5 sts; rep from * around, sl st in first dc to join. *(42 sts)*

Round 8: 1ch, 1dc in BLO of each st around, sl st in first dc to join.

Rounds 9–11: 1ch, 1dc in each st around, sl st in first dc to join.

Round 12: Change to yarn B. 1ch, 1dc in each st around, sl st in first dc to join.

Round 13: Change to yarn A. 1ch, 1dc in each st around, sl st in first dc to join.

Round 14: Change to yarn B. 1ch, 1dc in each st around, sl st in first dc to join.

Round 15: Change to yarn A. 1ch, 1dc in each st around, sl st in first dc to join.

Round 16: 1ch, 1dc in first 8 sts, 8ch, miss 5 sts, 1dc in next 16 sts, 8ch, miss 5 sts, 1dc in last 8 sts, sl st in first dc to join. *(2 handles made)*

Round 17: 1ch, 1dc in first 8 sts, work 8dc around 8ch from previous round, 1dc in next 16 sts, work 8dc around 8ch from previous round, 1dc in last 8 sts, sl st in first dc to join.

Fasten off.

Making Up and Finishing

Weave in all loose ends and gently steam block to measurements.

Having children means always having a lot of stuff to carry about, but I wanted an alternative to the big, old rucksack I usually keep everything in. This bag is a roomy, sturdy sack, that can hold everything I need but in a more 'hipsterish' way. Slung over my shoulder on the way to the park, it makes me feel less like a packhorse and more like a cool mom about town.

hipster holdall

Yarn

Katia Big Ribbon (super chunky weight; 50% cotton, 50% polyester; 72m/78yds per 200g/7oz ball)

- 2 balls of 08 Khaki (A)
- 2 balls of 03 Cream (B)

Hooks and Notions

10mm (US N/15) crochet hook

Tapestry needle

80cm (32in) length of 5cm (2in) wide jute/hessian upholstery tape

Sewing needle and matching thread

Tension

9 sts and 8 rows to 10cm (4in) measured over double crochet

Finished Size

35cm (13¾in) wide x 35cm (13¾in) deep

Abbreviations

See page 125.

Pattern Notes

The Chart is read from bottom to top and from right to left on every row.

For the Bag

Round 1: Using yarn A and 10mm (US N/15) hook, make a magic ring. Work 1ch (does not count as st throughout), 6dc into the ring, sl st in first dc to join. *(6 sts)*

Round 2: 1ch, 2dc in each st around, sl st in first dc to join. *(12 sts)*

Round 3: 1ch, *2dc in first st, 1dc in next st; rep from * to end, sl st in first dc to join. *(18 sts)*

Round 4: 1ch, *2dc in first st, 1dc in next 2 sts; rep from * to end, sl st in first dc to join. *(24 sts)*

Round 5: 1ch, *2dc in first st, 1dc in next 3 sts; rep from * to end, sl st in first dc to join. *(30 sts)*

Round 6: 1ch, *2dc in first st, 1dc in next 4 sts; rep from * to end, sl st in first dc to join. *(36 sts)*

Round 7: 1ch, *2dc in first st, 1dc in next 5 sts; rep from * to end, sl st in first dc to join. *(42 sts)*

Round 8: 1ch, *2dc in first st, 1dc in next 6 sts; rep from * to end, sl st in first dc to join. *(48 sts)*

Round 9: 1ch, *2dc in first st, 1dc in next 7 sts; rep from * to end, sl st in first dc to join. *(54 sts)*

Round 10: 1ch, *2dc in first st, 1dc in next 8 sts; rep from * to end, sl st in first dc to join. *(60 sts)*

Rounds 11–16: 1ch, 1dc in each st around, sl st in first dc to join.

Round 17: Change to yarn B. 1ch, 1dc in each st around, sl st in first dc to join.

Round 18: Change to yarn A. 1ch, 1dc in each st around, sl st in first dc to join.

Commence Tapestry Crochet pattern (see page 122) and work in dc changing colour as indicated and working stitches over the unused yarn as you go. The number indicates the amount of stitches and the letter denotes the yarn colour. For example; 5A, 4B, 5A means work 5dc in A, 4dc in B, 5dc in A. See Chart for reference.

Round 19: 1ch, *1B, 9A; rep from * to end, sl st in first dc to join.
Round 20: 1ch, *2B, 8A; rep from * to end, sl st in first dc to join.
Round 21: 1ch, *3B, 7A; rep from * to end, sl st in first dc to join.
Round 22: 1ch, *4B, 6A; rep from * to end, sl st in first dc to join.
Round 23: 1ch, *5B, 5A; rep from * to end, sl st in first dc to join.
Round 24: 1ch, *6B, 4A; rep from * to end, sl st in first dc to join.
Round 25: 1ch, *7B, 3A; rep from * to end, sl st in first dc to join.
Round 26: 1ch, *8B, 2A; rep from * to end, sl st in first dc to join.
Round 27: 1ch, *9B, 1A; rep from * to end, sl st in first dc to join.
Work with only one colour per round again as follows:
Round 28: Using yarn B only, 1ch, 1dc in each st around, sl st in first dc to join.
Round 29: Change to yarn A. 1ch, 1dc in each st around, sl st in first dc to join.
Round 30: Change to yarn B. 1ch, 1dc in each st around, sl st in first dc to join.
Round 31: 1ch, *dc2tog, 1dc in next 8 sts; rep from * to end, sl st in first dc to join. *(54 sts)*
Round 32: 1ch, *dc2tog, 1dc in next 7 sts; rep from * to end, sl st in first dc to join. *(48 sts)*
Round 33: 1ch, *dc2tog, 1dc in next 6 sts; rep from * to end, sl st in first dc to join. *(42 sts)*
Round 34: 1ch, *dc2tog, 1dc in next 5 sts; rep from * to end, sl st in first dc to join. *(36 sts)*
Fasten off.

Making Up and Finishing

Weave in all loose ends and gently steam block.

For the strap: Fold the ends of the upholstery tape over to create a hem, and sew to either side of the bag. Wrap lengths of yarn around each end of the strap, just above where it joins the bag, to decorate.

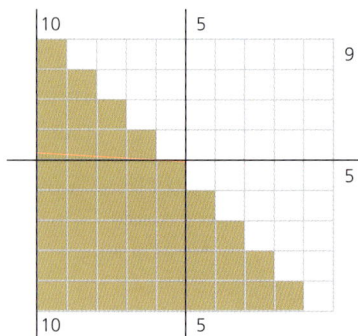

TIP Personalize your holdall by plaiting lengths of yarn around the whole length of the strap.

Key

■ Khaki (A)

□ Cream (B)

My youngest wanted a bag he could use to carry his books, pens and paper around in, so we sat down together and worked out the dimensions and an easy fastening he could use. We then went yarn shopping together and he jumped on the brightest and loudest yarn in the shop! So this bag was designed by a five year old but has been a big hit with kids of all ages on our street.

chunky envelope rucksack

Skill Level * * *

Yarn
Lion Brand Wool-Ease, Thick & Quick Prints (super chunky weight; 86% acrylic, 10% wool, 4% polyester; 80m/87yds per 140g/5oz ball)

   2 balls of 510 Toucan (A)

Lion Brand Heartland (Aran weight; 100% acrylic, 230m/251yds per 140g/5oz ball)

   1 ball of 151 Katmai (B)

Hooks and Notions
10mm (US N/15) crochet hook

5mm (US H/8) crochet hook

Locking stitch marker

Tapestry needle

Approx. 42cm (17¾in) square piece of lining fabric (plus seam allowance)

Sewing needle and matching thread

Pins

1 button, 3cm (1¼in) diameter

Tension
8 sts and 9 rows to 10cm (4in) measured over double crochet

Finished Size
35cm (13¾in) wide x 35cm (13¾in) deep

Abbreviations
See page 125.

For the Bag
Using yarn A and 10mm (US N/15) hook, make 31ch.

Row 1: 1dc in second ch from hook (missed ch does not count as st), 1dc in each ch to end, turn. *(30 sts)*

Rows 2–35: 1ch (does not count as st throughout), 1dc in each st to end, turn.

Fasten off.

Edging round: Using 5mm (US H/8) hook, join yarn B in one side st, 1ch, then work 2dc in every st and row end around, working 4dc in each corner, join with sl st in first dc. Fasten off.

TIP When a project uses yarns of two different thicknesses, try and pick one that uses a hook half the size of the other. That way you know you will be able to work 2 smaller stitches to every large one.

For the Straps (make 2 alike)

Using yarn B and 5mm (US H/8) hook, make 71ch.

Round 1: 2dc in second ch from hook (missed ch does not count as st), 1dc in next 68 ch, 3dc in end ch. Working up the other side of the ch, 1dc in next 68 ch, 1dc in end ch, join with a sl st in first dc, place marker for beginning of round. *(142 sts)*

Round 2: 1ch, 2dc in each of first 2 sts, 1dc in next 68 sts, 2dc in each of next 3 sts, 1dc in next 68 sts, 2dc in last st, join with a sl st in first dc. *(148 sts)*

Fasten off leaving a long tail for sewing the straps to the rucksack.

Making Up and Finishing

Weave in loose ends of rucksack panel and block.

Cut the lining fabric to the same size as the rucksack panel. Hem the edges of the lining, pin in place and stitch to reverse side of the bag panel noting that there will be a small gap between the edge of the lining and the edge of the bag. Fold three corners into the middle to make an envelope shape. Using yarn B, whip stitch (see page 118) the two bottom diagonal edges together.

Using yarn B and 5mm (US H/8) hook, join yarn to tip of opening flap, work 10ch and fasten off. Secure the tail in place to make a button loop. Stitch button in place.

Stitch ends of straps in place on each side on the back of the rucksack.

This tote can go literally anywhere, at any time of the day or night, and is super quick and easy to make. The monochrome colourway with a bit of glitzy gold and a flash of bright lining, when teamed with a pair of pedal pushers and ruby red pumps, make me feel like Audrey Hepburn!

maxi striped tote

Yarn

Hoooked Zpagetti (super chunky weight; 100% recycled jersey fabric; 120m/131yds per 850g/30oz cone)

- 1 cone of Black (A)
- 1 cone of White (B)

Hooks and Notions

10mm (US N/15) crochet hook

Tapestry needle

Approx. 35cm x 80cm (13¾in x 31½in) piece of lining fabric

1m (40in) long, 3.5cm (1½in) wide gold leather or leather-look strap

Sewing needle and matching thread

Tension

7 sts and 3 rows to 10cm (4in) measured over double crochet

Finished Size

34cm (13½in) wide x 40cm (16in) deep

Abbreviations

See page 125.

Pattern Notes

As the tote is lined there is no need to fasten off each colour change; simply carry the yarn loosely up the inside of the bag.

For the Tote

Using yarn A and 10mm (US N/15) hook, make 29ch.

Round 1: 4tr in fourth ch from hook (missed 3ch counts as 1tr), 1tr in next 24 ch, 5tr in end ch. Working up the other side of the ch, 1tr in next 24 ch, sl st in top of beginning 3ch to join. (*58 sts*)

Round 2: 3ch (counts as 1tr throughout), 1tr in each st around, sl st in third ch of beginning 3ch to join.

Round 3: Change to yarn B. 3ch, 1tr in each st around, sl st in third ch of beginning 3ch to join.

Round 4: Change to yarn A. 3ch, 1tr in each st around, sl st in third ch of beginning 3ch to join.

Rounds 5–10: Rep Rounds 3–4.

Round 11: Rep Round 3.

Round 12: Using yarn B, 1ch, 1dc in each st around, sl st in first dc to join. Fasten off.

Making Up and Finishing

Weave in all loose ends and gently steam block.

Cut the gold leather or leather-look strap into two 20in (50cm) lengths and sew straps in place using the photographs for guidance.

For the ridges: Join yarn B around the post of any tr in a yarn B stripe. Work 1dc around the post of each tr stitch in the same yarn B row travelling perpendicular to the direction the tote was crocheted in. Slip stitch in first dc to join and fasten off. Repeat for each yarn B row.

Sew the lining and attach to inside of the tote.

TIP Play with colours for the yarn, strap, and lining – subtle pastels, clashing neons, or fruity brights will change the look of this tote in a flash.

I have a confession: I'm completely obsessed with tassels! This bag uses a bulky cotton yarn, which is ideal for turning into tassels and fringing as it doesn't stretch or fray, simply becoming beautifully soft and all the more tactile.

tassel tote

Skill Level ✳ ✳ ✳

Yarn

DMC Natura XL Just Cotton (super bulky weight; 100% cotton, 75m/82yds per 100g/3½oz ball)

- 1 ball of 92 yellow (A)
- 1 ball of 10 dark orange (B)
- 1 ball of 06 burgundy (C)
- 2 balls of 71 blue (D)
- 1 ball of 73 grey-white (E)

Hooks and Notions

6mm (US J/10) crochet hook

Tapestry needle

104cm (41in) length of 2cm (¾in) wide brown belt or strap

Sewing needle and gold embroidery thread

2cm (¾in) jump ring

Decorative feather and belt clip (optional)

Tension

12 sts and 13 rows to 10cm (4in) measured over double crochet after blocking

Finished Size

22cm (8¾in) x 30cm (11¾in)

Abbreviations

See page 125.

For the Bag

Using yarn A and 6mm (US J/10) hook, make 26ch.

Row 1: 1dc in second ch from hook (missed ch does not count as st), 1dc in each ch to end, turn. (*25 sts*)

Row 2: Using yarn B, 1ch (does not count as st throughout), 1dc in each st, turn.

Row 3: Using yarn C, 1ch, 1dc in each st, turn.

Row 4: Using yarn D, 1ch, 1dc in each st, turn.

Row 5: Using yarn E, 1ch, 1dc in each st, turn.

Rows 6–7: Using yarn D, 1ch, 1dc in each st, turn.

Commence Tapestry Crochet pattern (see page 122) and work in dc changing colour as indicated and working stitches over the unused yarn as you go. The number indicates the amount of stitches and the letter denotes the yarn colour. For example; 5A, 4B, 5A means work 5dc in A, 4dc in B, 5dc in A. See Chart for reference.

Row 8: 12D, 1A, 12D, turn.

Row 9: 11D, 3A, 11D, turn.

Row 10: 10D, 5A, 10D, turn.

Row 11: 9D, 3A, 1B, 3A, 9D, turn.

Row 12: 8D, 3A, 3B, 3A, 8D, turn.

Row 13: 7D, 3A, 5B, 3A, 7D, turn.

Row 14: 6D, 3A, 3B, 1C, 3B, 3A, 6D, turn.

Row 15: 5D, 3A, 3B, 3C, 3B, 3A, 5D, turn.

Row 16: 4D, 3A, 3B, 5C, 3B, 3A, 4D, turn.

Row 17: 3D, 3A, 3B, 3C, 1E, 3C, 3B, 3A, 3D, turn.

Row 18: 2D, 3A, 3B, 3C, 3E, 3C, 3B, 3A, 2D, turn.

Row 19: 3D, 3A, 3B, 3C, 1E, 3C, 3B, 3A, 3D, turn.

Row 20: 4D, 3A, 3B, 5C, 3B, 3A, 4D, turn.

Row 21: 5D, 3A, 3B, 3C, 3B, 3A, 5D, turn.

Row 22: 6D, 3A, 3B, 1C, 3B, 3A, 6D, turn.

Row 23: 7D, 3A, 5B, 3A, 7D, turn.

Row 24: 8D, 3A, 3B, 3A, 8D, turn.

Row 25: 9D, 3A, 1B, 3A, 9D, turn.

Row 26: 10D, 5A, 10D, turn.

Row 27: 11D, 3A, 11D, turn.

Row 28: 12D, 1A, 12D, turn.

Now work with one colour per row as follows:

Rows 29–30: Using yarn D, 1ch, 1dc in each st, turn.
Row 31: Using yarn E, 1ch, 1dc in each st, turn.
Row 32: Using yarn D, 1ch, 1dc in each st, turn.
Row 33: Using yarn C, 1ch, 1dc in each st, turn.
Row 34: Using yarn B, 1ch, 1dc in each st, turn.
Row 35: Using yarn A, 1dc in each st to end, turn.
Row 36: Using yarn A, 1ch, 1dc BLO in each st, turn.
Row 37: Using yarn B, 1dc in each st to end, turn.
Rows 38–40: Rep Rows 3–5.
Row 41: Using yarn A, 1dc in each st to end, turn.
Rows 42–46: Rep Rows 2–6.
Rows 47–67: Using yarn D, 1dc in each st to end, turn.
Rows 68–72: Rep Rows 31–35.
Fasten off.

Making Up and Finishing

Weave in loose ends and block to measurements.

Using gold embroidery thread, whip stitch (see page 118) the sides together.

For the tassel: Cut 2 x 25cm (9¾in) lengths of each yarn A–E. Fold in half around a 2cm (¾in) jump ring and bind the top 2cm (¾in) with gold embroidery thread. Add any other decorations to the jump ring that you like – I used a feather shape cut from a piece of scrap leather.

To attach the handle: Cut the buckle off the belt and using an awl, make a hole in each end. Attach to the bag on the third row down, using a length of matching coloured yarn – make sure you slip the jump ring with your decorations over the belt before stitching it down.

For the fringing: Cut 25 x 20cm (8in) lengths of yarn E and thread each one through a stitch along the bottom of the bag by making a loop, posting it through the stitch and pulling it back through itself (see Tassels and fringes, page 120).

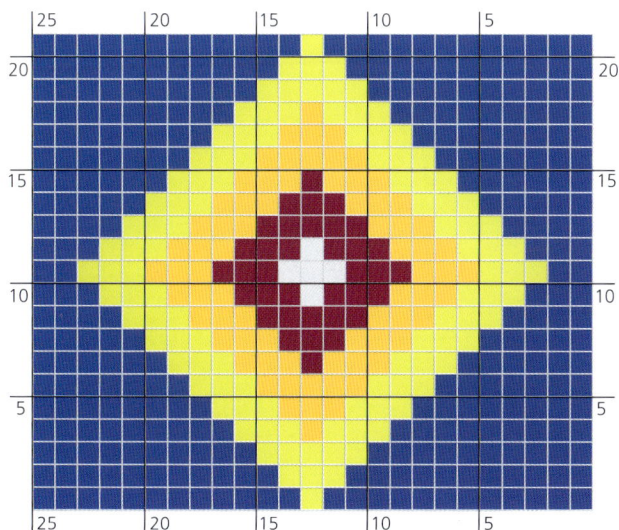

Key

◻ yellow (A)	
◻ dark orange (B)	
◻ burgundy (C)	
◻ blue (D)	
◻ grey-white (E)	

This tote is an elegant take on the traditional string shopping bag. Still nice and roomy, with a bit of stretch, it makes a chic replacement for when you head off to the grocery shop.

chic shopping tote

Skill Level ✶ ✶ ✶

Yarn
Katia Big Ribbon (super chunky weight; 50% cotton, 50% polyester; 72m/77yds per 200g/7oz ball)

    2 balls of 13 Blue (A)
    1 ball of 03 Cream (B)

Hooks and Notions
10mm (US N/15) crochet hook

Tapestry needle

1m (1yd) of 2.5cm (1in) wide cotton canvas tape

Sewing needle and matching thread

Tension
8 sts and 5 rows to 10cm (4in) measured over pattern

Finished Size
30cm (11¾in) wide x 35cm (13¾in) deep

22cm (8½in) handle drop

Abbreviations
See page 125.

Pattern Notes
Adjust the hook size up or down a size to create a stretchier or firmer fabric.

For the Tote Panels (make 2 alike)
Using yarn A and 10mm (US N/15) hook, make 26ch.

Row 1: 1dc in second ch from hook (missed ch does not count as st), *miss 2 ch, [(1tr, 1ch) 4 times, 1tr] in next ch, miss 2 ch, 1dc in next ch; rep from * to end, turn.

Row 2: 5ch (counts as 1tr and 2ch throughout), miss next 2 tr, 1dc in centre tr of fan from previous row, *2ch, miss next 2 tr, 1tr in dc from previous row, 2ch, miss next 2 tr, 1dc in centre tr of fan from previous row; rep from * to end, 2ch, miss last 2tr, 1tr in last dc, turn.

Row 3: 1ch (does not count as st throughout), 1dc in first tr, *[(1tr, 1ch) 4 times, 1tr] in next dc from previous row, 1dc in next tr from previous row; rep from * to end, working final dc in third ch of previous row, turn.

Rows 4–16: Rep Rows 2–3, finishing with Row 2.

Row 17: Change to yarn B. 1ch (does not count as st), 1dc in first tr, *2dc in 2ch-sp, 1dc in next dc, 2dc in 2ch-sp, 1dc in next tr; rep from * to end, working final dc in third ch of previous row.
Fasten off.

Making Up and Finishing
Weave in loose ends and gently block.

Using a length of yarn A, join the sides and bottom of the bag together using whip stitch (see page 118).

Make the handles as follows: Cut 2 x 50cm (19¾in) lengths of canvas tape, and sew to the top inner edges of the bag.

This pattern is a great way of using up any odds and ends of yarn you have and is the perfect excuse to mix and match colours. I think it would look amazing in red, white, and black, but it could be equally striking in full rainbow hues. Either way, it's just perfect for tucking your WIP into and trotting off for a coffee, catch-up, and crochet-a-long with friends.

granny square tote

Yarn

Cascade Pacific (Aran weight; 60% cotton, 40% Merino wool, 195m/213yds per 100g/3½oz ball)

  1 ball of shade 02 White (A)
  1 ball of shade 52 Geranium (B)
  1 ball of shade 40 Peacock (C)

Jarol Heritage DK (light worsted weight; 55% wool, 25% acrylic, 20% nylon, 250m/273yds per 100g/3½oz ball)

  1 ball of shade 140 Gold (D)

Hooks and Notions

4mm (US G/6) crochet hook

Tapestry needle

Plastic hoop bag handles, 13cm (5¼in) diameter

Approx. 28cm x 63.5cm (11in x 25in) piece of lining fabric

Sewing needle and matching thread

Finished Size

26cm (10¼in) wide x 31cm (12¼in) deep

Tension

1 Small Square to measure 8.5cm (3½in)

Abbreviations

See page 125.

For the Small Squares

For Square 1

Using yarn D and 4mm (US G/6) hook, make 5ch, sl st in first ch to form a ring.

Round 1: 3ch (counts as 1tr throughout), 15tr into the ring, sl st in third ch of 3ch to join. *(16 sts)*

Round 2: Change to yarn B. 3ch, 1tr in same st, 2tr in each st to end, sl st in third ch of 3ch to join. *(32 sts)*

Round 3: Change to yarn A. 3ch, 1tr in same st, *1htr in next st, 1dc in each of next 4 sts, 1htr in next st, 2tr in next st, 2ch, 2tr in next st; rep from * twice more, 1htr in next st, 1dc in each of next 4 sts, 1htr in next st, 2tr in next st, 2ch, sl st in third ch of 3ch to join.

Round 4: Change to yarn C. 3ch, *1tr in each st to ch-sp, [2tr, 2ch, 2tr] in ch-sp; rep from * a further 3 times, sl st in third ch of 3ch to join.
Fasten off.
Repeat to make 4 more squares in the following yarn sequences:

For Square 2

Starting Chain and Round 1: Yarn B.
Round 2: Yarn D.
Round 3: Yarn A.
Round 4: Yarn C.

TIP This pattern uses granny squares of different sizes joined together to form a rectangle. Using one colour as the dominant, outer edge round brings consistency to the overall look, but changing the order of the inner colours brings interest and fun to the design.

For the Medium Square (make 1)

Using preferred colour sequence, work as for Small Square then continue as follows:

Rounds 5–8: Rep Round 4 changing colours as desired but ensuring you use yarn C for final round.

For the Large Square (make 1)

Work as for Medium Square but repeat Round 4 a further four times (12 rounds in total), ensuring you use yarn C for final round.

Making Up and Finishing

Weave in all loose ends and gently block.

Lay the Large Square flat and position three Small Squares vertically down the right-hand side. Place the Medium Square to the bottom left-hand corner of Large Square and position two Small Squares along the top of it.

Sew all squares together using whip stitch (see page 118) and working through back loops only (BLO), then sew the sides together to form a tube.

Rejoin yarn C at the bottom edge of bag.

Round 1: 3ch, 1tr in each st around, sl st in top of 3ch to join. Repeat Round 1 once more. Fasten off.

Sew the bottom edge closed. To square off the corners, turn the tote inside out, fold over each bottom corner approx. 3cm (1¼in), and tack the corner point to the bottom seam. Turn right side out again.

Rejoin yarn C at the top edge.
Round 1: 3ch, 1tr in each stitch around, sl st in top of 3ch to join.
Round 2: Change to yarn B. 1ch (does not count as st), 1dc in each st to end, sl st in first dc to join.
Round 3: Change to yarn D. 1ch, 1dc in each st to end, sl st in first dc to join.
Round 4: Change to yarn C. 3ch, 1tr in each st to end, sl st in top of 3ch to join.
Fasten off.

For the handles: Using yarn C and 4mm (US G/6) hook, work dc around hoop handles until they are tightly covered. Sew to top of bag.

For the lining: Sew the sides of the lining fabric together and square off the bottom corners. Hem the top edge and hand sew the lining into the bag.

For Square 3
Starting Chain and Round 1: Yarn A.
Round 2: Yarn B.
Round 3: Yarn D.
Round 4: Yarn C.

For Square 4
Starting Chain and Round 1: Yarn D.
Round 2: Yarn A.
Round 3: Yarn B.
Round 4: Yarn C.

For Square 5
Starting Chain and Round 1: Yarn B.
Round 2: Yarn D.
Round 3: Yarn A.
Round 4: Yarn C.

For me, polka dots evoke the 1950s and this satchel provided the perfect excuse to use some vintage fabric I've had squirrelled away for ages, to make the lining and strap.

spotty satchel

Skill Level ✳ ✳ ✳

Yarn

Caron Simply Soft Party (Aran weight; 99% acrylic, 1% polyester; 150m/164yd per 85g/3oz ball)

  3 balls of 0004 Teal Sparkle (A)
  2 balls of 0001 Snow Sparkle (B)

Hooks and Notions

4mm (US G/6) crochet hook

Tapestry needle

Approx. 26cm x 60.5cm (10¼in x 23¾in) piece of lining fabric plus approx. 6.5cm x 100.5cm (2½in x 39½in) length for strap

2 D-rings, 3cm (1¼in) across

2 buttons, 2.5cm (1in) diameter

Tension

16 sts and 9 rows to 10cm (4in) measured over double crochet

Finished Size

25cm (9¾in) deep x 30cm (11¾in) wide

Abbreviations

See page 125.

Special Stitches

tr2tog: [Yrh, insert hook in **next** st, pull up a loop, yrh, pull through 2 loops] 2 times (3 loops on hook), yrh, pull through all loops on hook (1 loop on hook).

tr5tog: [Yrh, insert hook in **next** st, pull up a loop, yrh, pull through 2 loops] 5 times (6 loops on hook), yrh, pull through all loops on hook (1 loop on hook).

Pattern Notes

The body of this bag is worked in the round with the flap then worked in rows.

For the Satchel

Using yarn A and 4mm (US G/6) hook, make 120ch, sl st in first ch to join in the round taking care not to twist the ch.

Round 1: 3ch (counts as 1tr throughout), 1tr in each ch around, sl st in third ch of 3ch to join. *(120 sts)*

Round 2: 3ch, 2tr in same st, miss 2 sts, 1dc in next st, *miss 2 sts, 5tr in next st, miss 2 sts, 1dc in next st; rep from * around, miss 2 sts, 2tr in same st as 2tr at beginning of round, sl st in top of beginning 3ch to join.

Round 3: 1ch (does not count as st throughout), 1dc in first st, 2ch, tr5tog, *2ch, 1dc in third tr of 5tr from previous row, 2ch, work tr5tog, 2ch; rep from * around, sl st in first dc to join.

Round 4: 1ch, *1dc in next st, miss 2 ch, 5tr in next st, miss 2 ch; rep from * around, sl st in first dc to join.

Round 5: Using yarn B for the 2nd, 6th, 10th, 14th, 18th tr5tog, 3ch, miss first dc, tr2tog, 2ch, 1dc in third tr of 5tr from previous row, *2ch, tr5tog, 2ch, 1dc in third tr of 5tr; rep from * to last 2 sts, 2ch, tr2tog inserting hook through centre of first tr2tog of round before final pull through.

Round 6: Using yarn B for the 2nd, 6th, 10th, 14th and 18th 5tr, 3ch, 2tr in same st, miss 2 ch, 1dc in next st, *miss 2 ch, 5tr in next st, miss 2 ch, 1dc in next st; rep from * around, miss 2 ch, 2tr in same st as 2tr at beginning of round, sl st in top of beginning 3ch to join.

Round 7: Using yarn A only, rep Round 3.

Round 8: Using yarn A only, rep Round 4.

Round 9: Rep Round 5 using yarn B for the 4th, 8th, 12th, 16th, and 20th tr5tog.

Round 10: Rep Round 6 using yarn B for the 4th, 8th, 12th, 16th, and 20th 5tr.

Round 11: Using yarn A only, rep Round 3

Round 12: Using yarn A only, rep Round 4.

Rounds 13–20: Rep Rounds 5–12.

Round 21–24: Rep Round 5–8.

Round 25: Using yarn A only, rep Round 5.

Now work in rows to create the flap as follows:

Row 1: 3ch, [2tr in 2ch-sp, 1tr in next st] 16 times, turn.

Rows 2–11: 3ch, 1tr in each st to end, turn.

Row 12: 1ch, 1dc in next 5 sts, 5ch, miss 4 sts, 1dc in each st to last 9 sts, 5ch, miss 4 sts, 1dc in last 5 sts, turn. *(2 buttonholes made)*

Row 13: 3ch, 1tr in each st across working 4tr in each 4ch-sp.

Fasten off.

Making Up and Finishing

Weave in ends and block to measurements.

Sew the bottom edge closed. To square off the corners, turn the satchel inside out, fold over each bottom corner approx. 3cm (1¼in), and tack the corner point to the bottom seam. Turn right side out again.

Sew buttons in place to correspond with the buttonholes made in Row 12.

Using a length of yarn A, thread the tapestry needle and attach a D-ring to either side of the bag.

With right-sides together, fold the 100.5cm (39½in) length of lining fabric in half lengthways and seam the long edge. Pull out the right way, tuck in and hem the ends, then loop around the D-rings and sew together.

Hem both short ends of the larger piece of fabric. With right-sides together, fold over approx. 30cm (11¾in) of the fabric (ensure it's not the end with the buttonholes in) and sew the side seams. Insert into the bag, and hand sew to the top edge of the bag under the scalloped border. Fold under the raw edges of the lining for the bag flap, and pin into place on the inside of the flap Take care to ensure the buttonholes are not covered, and hand sew the lining in place.

This little bag was inspired by the bright variegated yarn, and the cables in the pattern really bring the colours alive, making a striking, bold design.

tote-ally hot

Yarn

Lion Brand Unique (chunky weight; 100% acrylic; 100m/109yds per 100g/3½oz ball)

   1 ball of shade 210 Circus (A)

Lion Brand Heartland (Aran weight; 100% acrylic, 230m/251yds per 142g/5oz ball)

   1 ball of shade 151 Katmai (B)

Hooks and Notions

6mm (US J/10) crochet hook

Tapestry needle

Approx. 21.5cm x 43cm (8½in x 17in) piece of lining fabric

Sewing needle and matching thread

Tension

15 sts x 9 rows to 10cm (4in) measured over cable pattern

Finished Size

20cm (8in) wide x 21cm (8¼in) deep (not including handles)

Abbreviations

See page 125.

For the Tote Panel (make 2 alike)

Using yarn A and 6mm (US J/10) hook, make 27ch.

Row 1 (RS): 1dc in second ch from hook (missed ch does not count as st), 1dc in each ch to end, turn. *(26 sts)*

Row 2 (WS): 3ch (counts as first tr), *miss 2 sts, 1tr in next 2 sts, 1tr in first miss st, 1tr in second miss st; rep from * to last st, 1tr in last st, turn.

Row 3: 1ch (does not count as st throughout), 1dc in each st to end, turn.

Rows 4–17: Rep Rows 3–4.

Fasten off.

With RS facing, join yarn B at top right-hand corner.

Round 1: 1ch, *3dc in corner, 1dc in each st to next corner, 3dc in corner, 2dc around each row end to corner; rep from * once more, join with a sl st in first dc.

Rounds 2–3: 1ch, 1dc in each st around, working 2dc in each corner, join with a sl st in first dc.

Fasten off.

Weave in loose ends and gently block both panels to measurements.

For the Handles

Thread the tapestry needle with a length of yarn B and using whip stitch (see page 118), sew the panels together along three sides leaving the short top edge open.

Join yarn B at top right-hand corner.

Round 1: 1ch, 1dc in next 6 sts, 25ch, miss 16 sts, 1dc in next 12 sts, 25ch, miss 16 sts, 1dc in next 6 sts, sl st in first dc to join. *(2 handles made)*

Round 2: 1ch, 1dc in next 6 sts, 26dc in 25ch-sp, 1dc in next 12 sts, 26dc in 25ch-sp, 1dc in next 6 sts, sl st in first dc to join.

Rounds 3–4: 1ch, 1dc in each st around, sl st in first dc to join.

Fasten off.

Making Up and Finishing

Weave in remaining loose ends.

Sew the sides of the lining fabric together and square off the bottom corners. Hem the top edge and hand sew the lining into the bag.

chapter 2 bags and handbags

This pattern was actually inspired by someone's sweater! Poor lady, I was following her around the playground at school pick-up time trying to snap a surreptitious picture on my phone. It was absolutely worth it though as this design goes with almost any look and is perfect for throwing all your essentials in before dashing out of the house.

blue block bag

Yarn

Jarol Heritage DK (DK weight; 55% wool, 25% acrylic, 20% nylon; 250m/273yds per 100g/3½oz ball)

  1 ball of 112 Black (A)
  1 ball of 100 Cream (B)
  1 ball of 136 Kingfisher (C)

Hooks and Notions

4mm (US G/6) crochet hook

Tapestry needle

91.5cm (36in) long leather strap

Awl

Linen thread

Sewing needle and matching thread

Approx. 33cm x 62cm (13in x 24½in) piece of lining fabric (optional)

Tension

22 sts and 21 rows to 10cm (4in) measured over double crochet

Finished Size

32cm (12½in) x 30.5cm (12in)

Abbreviations

See page 125.

Pattern Notes

The Chart is read from bottom to top and from right to left on every row.

For the Bag

Using yarn A, 4mm (US G/6) hook, and leaving a long tail, make 121ch.

Set-up round: 1dc in second ch from hook (missed ch does not count as st), 1dc in each ch to end, taking care not to twist the ch join with sl st in first dc to make a round and change to yarn B on final pull-through. *(120 sts)*

Commence Tapestry Crochet pattern (see page 122) and work in dc changing colour as indicated and working stitches over the unused yarn as you go. The number indicates the amount of stitches and the letter denotes the yarn colour. For example; 5A, 4B, 5A means work 5dc in A, 4dc in B, 5dc in A. See Chart for reference.

Round 1: 1ch (does not count as st throughout), *1B, 7A; rep from * to end, sl st in first dc to join.

Round 2: 1ch, *2B, 6A; rep from * to end, sl st in first dc to join.

Round 3: 1ch, *3B, 5A; rep from * to end, sl st in first dc to join.

Round 4: 1ch, *4B, 4A; rep from * to end, sl st in first dc to join.

Round 5: 1ch, *5B, 3A; rep from * to end, sl st in first dc to join.

Round 6: 1ch, *6B, 2A; rep from * to end, sl st in first dc to join.

Round 7: 1ch, *7B, 1A; rep from * to end, sl st in first dc to join.

Rounds 8–21: Rep Rounds 1–7 twice more.

Rounds 22–60: Join yarn C and continuing to work over either yarn A or B to maintain an even tension and breaking the one not in use, work 1ch, then 1dc in each st around, sl st in first dc to join.

Fasten off.

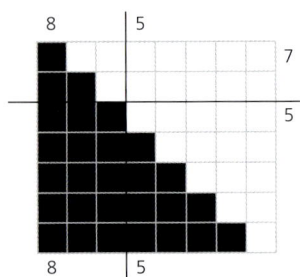

Key

■ Black (A)

□ White (B)

TIP Working tapestry crochet in the round will make the triangle pattern 'lean' to one side, to look like zigzags.

Making Up and Finishing

Weave in all loose ends and gently steam block.

Flatten the bag and whip stitch (see page 118) the bottom edges together, using the long foundation chain tail to close the small gap at start of the first round.

Sew the bottom edge closed. To square off the corners, turn the tote inside out, fold over each bottom corner approx. 3cm (1¼in) and tack the corner point to the bottom seam.

Turn right side out again.

Sew the sides of the lining fabric together and square off the bottom corners. Hem the top edge and hand sew the lining into the bag.

Using the awl, make 4 holes at each end of the leather strap. Use the linen thread to sew each end of the strap to one side of the bag – linen thread is really strong and won't snap so it's great for securing handles.

If you are as obsessive about co-ordinating outfits as I am, then this pattern is definitely for you! If you've got a party to go to at the weekend and can't find a handbag to match, this very cool, statement clutch is a fantastically quick make. Just grab some jersey yarn in a shade to match your outfit and in a couple of hours you'll have just what you need to complete your look!

party clutch

Skill Level ★ ☆ ☆

Yarn

Hoooked Zpagetti (super chunky weight; 100% recycled jersey fabric; 120m/131yds per 850g/30oz cone)

1 cone of mixed pattern (A)
Small quantity of contrasting colour (B)

Hooks and Notions

12mm (US P) crochet hook

Tapestry needle

1 button, 2.5cm (1in) diameter

Sewing needle and matching thread

Tension

6 sts and 7 rows to 10cm (4in) measured over double crochet

Finished Size

34cm (13½in) x 19cm (7½in)

Abbreviations

See page 125.

Pattern Notes

The Hoooked Zpagetti yarn used in this project is recycled from fashion industry remnants. This means you might not be able to find the same pattern or colour as shown, but there will be all sorts of amazing alternatives!

For the Bag

Using yarn A and 12mm (US P) hook, make 20ch.

Round 1: 1dc in second ch from hook (missed ch does not count as st), 1dc in next 17 ch, 3dc in end ch. Working up the other side of the ch, 1dc in next 17 ch, 2dc in end ch, sl st in first dc to join. *(40 sts)*

Rounds 2–13: 1ch, 1dc in each st around, sl st in first dc to join.

Do not fasten off but now work in rows to shape the front flap as follows:

Row 1: 1ch (does not count as st throughout), 1dc in next 20 sts, turn. *(20 sts)*

Row 2: 1ch, dc2tog, 1dc in next 16 sts, dc2tog, turn. *(18 sts)*

Row 3: 1ch, dc2tog, 1dc in next 14 sts, dc2tog, turn. *(16 sts)*

Row 4: 1ch, dc2tog, 1dc in next 12 sts, dc2tog, turn. *(14 sts)*

Row 5: 1ch, dc2tog, 1dc in next 10 sts, dc2tog, turn. *(12 sts)*

Row 6: 1ch, dc2tog, 1dc in next 8 sts, dc2tog, turn. *(10 sts)*

Row 7: 1ch, dc2tog, 1dc in next 6 sts, dc2tog, turn. *(8 sts)*

Row 8: 1ch, dc2tog, 1dc in next 4 sts, dc2tog, turn. *(6 sts)*

Row 9: 1ch, dc2tog, 1dc in next 2 sts, dc2tog, turn. *(4 sts)*

Row 10: 1ch, [dc2tog] twice. *(2 sts)*

Fasten off.

Making Up and Finishing

Weave in all loose ends and block to measurements.

Using yarn B and 12mm US P) hook, join yarn to the right-hand, inner corner of the edge of the bag. Work 1ch, then 1dc in each st all the way around the edge of the flap and opening of the bag, sl st in first dc to join.

Weave in any remaining loose ends. Sew button onto the front of the bag and use a gap in between the border stitches to push the button through and fasten the clutch.

TIPS

• This is a great project for new crocheters to practise double crochet stitches, learn decreases, and become accustomed to working both in the round and flat in rows – consider it a crochet workout!

• Remember to work the first dc into the stitch at the base of the 1ch to keep stitch counts correct and the edges nice and straight.

This bag is the reason I learned tapestry crochet. I'd had the design in my head for so long and all the other techniques I'd tried just weren't working. The tapestry method is ideal as it makes a dense fabric, and gives a great finish to the totally cool design. This bag is my favourite size to carry around – you can get a book, phone, keys, wallet and a drink in it, throw it over your shoulder and head off wherever the day may take you.

aztec shoulder bag

Skill Level ✲ ✲ ✲

Yarn

Jarol Heritage DK (DK weight; 55% wool, 25% acrylic, 20% nylon; 250m/273yds per 100g/3½oz ball)

1 ball of 140 Gold (A)
1 ball of 150 Spice (B)
1 ball of 133 Cerise (C)
1 ball of 137 Lime (D)

Small quantity of metallic yarn to crochet the edges together

Hooks and Notions

4mm (US G/6) crochet hook

Tapestry needle

1m (40in) long, 1.5cm (½in) wide leather or leather-look strap

Approx. 32cm x 49.5cm (12½in x 19½in) piece of lining fabric

Sewing needle and matching thread

Tension

22 sts and 18 rows to 10cm (4in) measured over double crochet

Finished Size

30.5cm (12in) x 24cm (9½in)

Abbreviations

See page 125.

Pattern Notes

This pattern is worked by turning at the end of each row and working 1ch which does not count as a stitch.

The Chart is read from bottom to top and from right to left on RS (odd numbered rows) and left to right on WS (even numbered rows).

For the Bag

Using yarn A and 4mm (US G/6) hook, make 62ch.

Row 1: 1dc in second ch from hook (missed ch does not count as st), 1dc in each ch to end, turn. *(61 sts)*

Row 2: Change to yarn B. 1ch (does not count as st throughout), 1dc in each st to end, turn.

Row 3: Change to yarn C. 1ch, 1dc in each st to end, turn.

Row 4: Change to yarn D. 1ch, 1dc in each st to end, turn.

Rows 5–6: Change to yarn A. 1ch, 1dc in each st to end, turn.

Rows 7–8: Change to yarn B. 1ch, 1dc in each st to end, turn.

Rows 9–10: Change to yarn C. 1ch, 1dc in each st to end, turn.

Rows 11–12: Change to yarn D. 1ch, 1dc in each st to end, turn.

Rows 13–17: Change to yarn B. 1ch, 1dc in each st to end, turn.

Commence Tapestry Crochet pattern (see page 122) and work in dc changing colour as indicated and working stitches over the unused yarn as you go. The number indicates the amount of stitches and the letter denotes the yarn colour. For example: 5A, 4B, 5A means work 5dc in A, 4dc in B, 5dc in A. See Chart for reference starting with Row 18.

Row 18: 1ch, 20B, 21C, 20B, turn.

Row 19: 1ch, 19B, 23C, 19B, turn.
Row 20: 1ch, 18B, 25C, 18B, turn.
Row 21: 1ch, 18B, 4C, 17A, 4C, 18B, turn.
Row 22: 1ch, 19B, 4C, 15A, 4C, 19B, turn.
Row 23: 1ch, 20B, 4C, 13A, 4C, 20B, turn.
Row 24: 1ch, 21B, 4C, 11A, 4C, 21B, turn.
Row 25: 1ch, 14B, 12C, 9A, 12C, 14B, turn.
Row 26: 1ch, 12B, 15C, 7A, 15C, 12B, turn.
Row 27: 1ch, 11B, 4C, 31A, 4C, 11B, turn.
Row 28: 1ch, 12B, 4C, 29A, 4C, 12B, turn.
Row 29: 1ch, 13B, 4C, 27A, 4C, 13B, turn.
Row 30: 1ch, 14B, 4C, 25A, 4C, 14B, turn.
Row 31: 1ch, 7B, 12C, 23A, 12C, 7B, turn.
Row 32: 1ch, 5B, 15C, 21A, 15C, 5B, turn.
Row 33: 1ch, 4B, 4C, 45A, 4C, 4B, turn.
Row 34: 1ch, 5B, 4C, 43A, 4C, 5B, turn.
Row 35: 1ch, 6B, 4C, 41A, 4C, 6B, turn.
Row 36: 1ch, 7B, 4C, 39A, 4C, 7B, turn.
Row 37: 1ch, 2B, 10C, 37A, 10C, 2B, turn.
Row 38: Change to yarn C. 1ch, 13C, 35A, 13C, turn.
Row 39: 1ch, 4C, 18A, 17D, 18A, 4C, turn.
Row 40: Change to yarn B. 1ch, 1B, 4C, 18A, 15D, 18A, 4C, 1B, turn.

Row 68: 1ch, 18C, 4B, 17D, 4B, 18C, turn.
Row 69: 1ch, 18C, 25B, 18C, turn.
Row 70: 1ch, 19C, 23B, 19C, turn.
Row 71: 1ch, 20C, 21B, 20C, turn.
Rows 72–76: With yarn C, 1ch, 1dc in each st to end, turn.
Rows 77–78: Change to yarn A. 1ch, 1dc in each st to end, turn.
Rows 79–80: Change to yarn B. 1ch, 1dc in each st to end, turn.
Rows 81–82: Change to yarn C. 1ch, 1dc in each st to end, turn.
Rows 83–84: Change to yarn D. 1ch, 1dc in each st to end, turn.
Row 85: Change to yarn A. 1ch, 1dc in each st to end, turn.
Row 86: Change to yarn B. 1ch, 1dc in each st to end, turn.
Row 87: Change to yarn C. 1ch, 1dc in each st to end, turn.
Row 88: Change to yarn D. 1ch, 1dc in each st to end.
Fasten off.

Making Up and Finishing

Weave in all loose ends and gently block.

Fold the bag in half with wrong sides together. Using the metallic thread and 4mm (US G/6) hook, join the sides using double crochet working through corresponding stitches.

Sew the bottom edge closed. To square off the corners, turn the bag inside out, fold over each bottom corner approx. 3cm (1¼in) and tack the corner point to the bottom seam. Turn right side out again.

Attach the bag handles roughly 15cm (6in) apart. Sew the sides of the lining fabric together and square off the bottom corners. Hem the top edge and hand sew the lining into the bag.

Row 41: 1ch, 2B, 4C, 18A, 13D, 18A, 4C, 2B, turn.
Row 42: 1ch, 3B, 4C, 18A, 11D, 18A, 4C, 3B, turn.
Row 43: 1ch, 4B, 4C, 18A, 9D, 18A, 4C, 4B, turn.
Row 44: 1ch, 5B, 4C, 18A, 7D, 18A, 4C, 5B, turn.
Row 45: Change to yarn C. 1ch, 5C, 4B, 18D, 7A, 18D, 4B, 5C, turn.
Row 46: 1ch, 4C, 4B, 18D, 9A, 18D, 4B, 4C, turn.
Row 47: 1ch, 3C, 4B, 18D, 11A, 18D, 4B, 3C, turn.
Row 48: 1ch, 2C, 4B, 18D, 13A, 18D, 4B, 2C, turn.
Row 49: 1ch, 1C, 4B, 18D, 15A, 18D, 4B, 1C, turn.
Row 50: Change to yarn B, 1ch, 4B, 18D, 17A, 18D, 4B, turn.
Row 51: 1ch, 13B, 35D, 13B, turn.
Row 52: Change to yarn C. 1ch, 2C, 10B, 37D, 10B, 2C, turn.
Row 53: 1ch, 7C, 4B, 39D, 4B, 7C, turn.
Row 54: 1ch, 6C, 4B, 41D, 4B, 6C, turn.
Row 55: 1ch, 5C, 4B, 43D, 4B, 5C, turn.
Row 56: 1ch, 4C, 4B, 45D, 4B, 4C, turn.
Row 57: 1ch, 5C, 14B, 21D, 14B, 5C, turn.
Row 58: 1ch, 7C, 12B, 23D, 12B, 7C, turn.
Row 59: 1ch, 14C, 4B, 25D, 4B, 14C, turn.
Row 60: 1ch, 13C, 4B, 27D, 4B, 13C, turn.
Row 61: 1ch, 12C, 4B, 29D, 4B, 12C, turn.
Row 62: 1ch, 11C, 4B, 31D, 4B, 11C, turn.
Row 63: 1ch, 12C, 15B, 7D, 15B, 12C, turn.
Row 64: 1ch, 14C, 12B, 9D, 12B, 14C, turn.
Row 65: 1ch, 21C, 4B, 11D, 4B, 21C, turn.
Row 66: 1ch, 20C, 4B, 13D, 4B, 20C, turn.
Row 67: 1ch, 19C, 4B, 15D, 4B, 19C, turn.

> **TIP** Maintain an even tension by always working stitches over at least one strand of yarn, even when only one colour is being worked across the row.

Key to chart

- ▮ Gold (A)
- ▮ Spice (B)
- ▮ Cerise (C)
- ▮ Lime (D)
- ☐ dc in colour indicated

When I was in my twenties I used to get a lot of my inspiration for makes from pop culture. Now that I'm in my thirties and my time is focused around my little ones, I take a lot of inspiration from walks in the park, woods and fields around our house. All year there's something different to spot: coloured leaves, amazing blossoms, delicate feathers and many other treasures. We often come home with bits poking out of pockets and piled in our hands so this basket was made to remedy that. Its wide shape means you can pile up all your forest finds and, with handles on either side, you can easily open it up and rummage around.

foraging basket

Yarn

WelcomeYarn T-Shirt Yarn (super chunky weight; 100% upcycled reclaimed yarn; approx. 450g/16oz per cone)

- 1 cone of Rust (A)
- 1 cone of Pale Yellow (B)

Note: These yarns are often not given shade names, so just look for the nearest approximation

Hooks and Notions

10mm (US N/15) crochet hook

Tapestry needle

Tension

First 4 rounds to measure 11.5cm (4½in) diameter

Finished Size

28cm (11in) wide x 14cm (5½in) deep

Abbreviations

See page 125.

Pattern Notes

The height and sturdy structure of this basket is achieved by working into and around rings of chain stitches.

For the Basket

Using yarn A and 10mm (US N/15) hook, make a magic ring.

Round 1: 1ch (does not count as st throughout), 6dc into the ring, sl st in first dc to join. *(6 sts)*

Round 2: 1ch, 2dc in each st around, sl st in first dc to join. *(12 sts)*

Round 3: 1ch, *2dc in first st, 1dc in next st; rep from * to end, sl st in first dc to join. *(18 sts)*

Round 4: 1ch, *2dc in first st, 1dc in next 2 sts; rep from * to end, sl st in first dc to join. *(24 sts)*

Round 5: 1ch, 1dc in BLO of each st around, sl st in first dc to join.

For the following rounds you will make rings of chain stitches and work into and then around them to add structure to the basket.

Round 6: Do not fasten off. Work 30ch, sl st in first ch to join, 1ch (does not count as st), 1dc in each ch around (ring made). Working **around** the base ring and into the sts from Round 5, *2dc in first st of Round 5, 1dc in next 3 sts; rep from * to end encasing the ring, sl st in first dc to join. *(30 sts)*

TIP Adjust the depth of the basket by working only one of two of the 'ring' rounds (Rounds 7, 8 and 9), then miss to Round 10 to finish the basket off.

Round 7: Do not fasten off. Work 36ch, sl st in first ch to join, 1ch (does not count as st), 1dc in each ch around (ring made). Working **around** the base ring and into the sts from Round 6, *2dc in first st of Round 6, 1dc in next 4 sts; rep from * to end encasing the ring, sl st in first dc to join. *(36 sts)*

Round 8: Do not fasten off. Work 42ch, sl st in first ch to join, 1ch (does not count as st), 1dc in each ch around (ring made). Working **around** the base ring and into the sts from Round 7, *2dc in first st of Round 7, 1dc in next 5 sts; rep from * to end encasing the ring, sl st in first dc to join. *(42 sts)*

Round 9: Do not fasten off. Work 48ch, sl st in first ch to join, 1ch (does not count as st), 1dc in each ch around (ring made). Working **around** the base ring and into the sts from Round 8, *2dc in first st of Round 8, 1dc in next 6 sts; rep from * to end encasing the ring, sl st in first dc to join. *(48 sts)*

Round 10: Change to yarn B, and work 1ch (does not count as st), 1dc in each st around, sl st in first dc to join.
Do not fasten off but continue as follows to make the crocheted i-cord handles.

Step 1: Insert hook in next st along the edge of the basket, yrh and pull up a loop, insert hook in next st, yrh and pull up a loop. *(3 loops on hook)*

Step 2: Carefully unhook the first 2 loops (and because this is bulky yarn, you can slip them over a finger to keep them safe – I use the middle finger of my hook hand or just hold them tightly), yrh and pull through last loop on the hook. *(1 loop on hook)*

Step 3: Put next loop from your finger back on the hook, yrh and pull through this loop. *(2 loops on hook)*

Step 4: Put last loop back on your hook, yrh and pull through this loop. *(3 loops on hook)*

Rep Steps 2–4 a further 14 times, or to desired length. Sl st end of the handle to the edge of the basket.

Rejoin yarn to opposite edge and complete second handle in the same way.

Making Up and Finishing

Weave in all loose ends and gently steam block into shape.

This bag is so adorable it's almost unbearable! Just the right size for all your essentials – use it for a quick hop to the shops, or if you're anything like me, as an accessory to freshen up an outfit on a night out.

apple shoulder bag

Skill Level ★ ★ ☆

Yarn

Nako Vega Aran (Aran weight; 100% acrylic; 195m/213yds per 100g/3½oz ball)

1 ball of 10268 Leaf Green (A)
1 ball of 208 White (B)

Hooks and Notions

4mm (US G/6) crochet hook

Tapestry needle

20cm (8in) zip

1m (40in) length of 2.5cm (1in) wide brown cotton webbing

2 D-rings

15cm (6in) length of 1cm (⅜in) wide brown velvet ribbon

Sewing needle

Brown sewing thread

Pins

Scissors

Tension

20 sts and 22 rows to 10cm (4in) measured over double crochet

Finished Size

20cm (8in) diameter x 7cm (2¾in) deep
47cm (18½in) handle drop

Abbreviations

See page 125.

> **TIP** Don't be scared of putting in a zip – there is no right or wrong way of doing it. If it is fixed in place, and it works, then you've done it! This pattern has also been designed for maximum zip insertion easiness!

For the Front of the Bag

Using yarn B and 4mm (US G/6) hook, make a magic ring.

Round 1: 1ch (does not count as st throughout), 6dc into the ring, sl st in first dc to join. *(6 sts)*

Round 2: 1ch, 2dc in each st around, sl st in first dc to join. *(12 sts)*

Round 3: 1ch, *2dc in first st, 1dc in next st; rep from * to end, sl st in first dc to join. *(18 sts)*

Round 4: 1ch, *2dc in first st, 1dc in next 2 sts; rep from * to end, sl st in first dc to join. *(24 sts)*

Round 5: 1ch, *2dc in first st, 1dc in next 3 sts; rep from * to end, sl st in first dc to join. *(30 sts)*

Round 6: 1ch, *2dc in first st, 1dc in next 4 sts; rep from * to end, sl st in first dc to join. *(36 sts)*

Round 7: 1ch, *2dc in first st, 1dc in next 5 sts; rep from * to end, sl st in first dc to join. *(42 sts)*

Round 8: 1ch, *2dc in first st, 1dc in next 6 sts; rep from * to end, sl st in first dc to join. *(48 sts)*

Round 9: 1ch, *2dc in first st, 1dc in next 7 sts; rep from * to end, sl st in first dc to join. *(54 sts)*

Round 10: 1ch, *2dc in first st, 1dc in next 8 sts; rep from * to end, sl st in first dc to join. *(60 sts)*

Round 11: 1ch, *2dc in first st, 1dc in next 9 sts; rep from * to end, sl st in first dc to join. *(66 sts)*

Round 12: 1ch, *2dc in first st, 1dc in next 10 sts; rep from * to end, sl st in first dc to join. *(72 sts)*

Round 13: 1ch, *2dc in first st, 1dc in next 11 sts; rep from * to end, sl st in first dc to join. *(78 sts)*

Round 14: 1ch, *2dc in first st, 1dc in next 12 sts; rep from * to end, sl st in first dc to join. *(84 sts)*

Round 15: 1ch, *2dc in first st, 1dc in next 13 sts; rep from * to end, sl st in first dc to join. *(90 sts)*

Round 16: 1ch, *2dc in first st, 1dc in next 14 sts; rep from * to end, sl st in first dc to join. *(96 sts)*

Round 17: 1ch, *2dc in first st, 1dc in next 15 sts; rep from * to end, sl st in first dc to join. *(102 sts)*

Round 18: Change to yarn A. 1ch, *2dc in first st, 1dc in next 16 sts; rep from * to end, sl st in first dc to join. *(108 sts)*

Round 19: 1ch, *2dc in first st, 1dc in next 17 sts; rep from * to end, sl st in first dc to join. *(114 sts)*

Round 20: 1ch, *2dc in first st, 1dc in next 18 sts; rep from * to end, sl st in first dc to join. *(120 sts)*

Round 21: 1ch, 1dc in BLO of each st around, sl st in first dc to join.

Rounds 22–25: 1ch, 1dc in each st, sl st in first dc to join. Fasten off.

For the Back of the Bag

Work as for the Front, but only using yarn A throughout.

Making Up and Finishing

Weave in all loose ends and block to measurements.

Pin one side of the zip to the top inside edge of the front panel and hand-sew it into place. Pin the other side of the zip to the top inside edge of the back panel and hand-sew into place.

With right sides together, using a length of yarn A and beginning just before the end of the zip, whip stitch (see page 118) the two panels together ending just before the zip-pull. Tack the ends of the zip to the panel fabric to hold it in place. Turn right side out and using yarn A, sew the D-rings to either side. Use the webbing to make the strap by stitching either end around the D-rings.

To make the apple pips, cut two 1¼in (3cm) lengths of velvet ribbon. With scissors, shape the ends into rounded points and hand sew into place.

To make the stalk, cut 8cm (3¼in) length of ribbon, fold in half and stitch into place at the top of the bag.

This handbag was influenced by the changing colours during the very end of summer as it becomes autumn, when all of the berries in the hedgerows are bursting into life, and the first leaves are beginning to yellow at their tips. I love this time of year and wanted a way to carry a little of that with me, throughout the seasons – that's exactly what this beautiful handbag does.

berry handbag

Skill Level ✳ ✳ ✳

Yarn

Jarol Heritage DK (DK weight; 55% wool, 25% acrylic, 20% nylon; 250m/273yds per 100g/3½oz ball)

- 1 ball of 140 Gold (A)
- 1 ball of 150 Spice (B)
- 1 ball of 102 Wine (C)
- 1 ball of 135 Damson (D)
- 1 ball of 153 Burgundy (E)

Hooks and Notions

4mm (US G/6) crochet hook

1 set of 25cm (10in) wide bag handles – oval or pear shaped with a slot

Tapestry needle

Tension

18 sts and 8 rows to 10cm (4in) measured over double crochet

Finished Size

32cm (12½in) x 20cm (8in) excluding handle

Abbreviations

See page 125.

Special Stitches

tr3tog: [Yrh, insert hook in next st, pull up a loop, yrh, pull through 2 loops] 3 times (4 loops on hook), yrh, pull through all loops on hook (1 loop on hook).

tr7tog: [Yrh, insert hook in next st, pull up a loop, yrh, pull through 2 loops] 7 times (8 loops on hook), yrh, pull through all loops on hook (1 loop on hook).

Pattern Notes

Don't worry if you can't find the same handles. So long as the number of stitches you work around the slot in your handle is divisible by 6, the pattern will still work.

For the Handles

Row 1: Using yarn A, make a slip knot and place it on the 4mm (US G/6) hook. Put the hook through the slot of the first bag handle and work 60dc around the slot, turn. *(60 sts)*

Row 2: 3ch (counts as 1tr throughout), 1tr in each st across. Fasten off.

Repeat for the second handle, but do not fasten off at the end of Row 2 and continue as follows to join the handles and commence working in the round:

Set-up round: 6ch, 1dc in tr at the bottom of the first handle, work 1dc in each st across first handle, 6ch, 1dc in tr on the opposite edge of the other handle, 1dc in each st across second handle, sl st in first dc to join. *(120 sts + 2 sets of 6ch)*

For the Bag

Round 1: 3ch, 1tr in each st to end working 6tr around each of the 6ch from set-up round, sl st in third ch of 3ch to join. *(132 sts)*

Round 2: Change to yarn B. 1ch (does not count as st throughout), 1dc in each st around, sl st in first dc to join.

Round 3: Change to yarn C. 1ch, 1dc in each st around, sl st in first dc to join.
Round 4: Change to yarn D. 1ch, 1dc in each st around, sl st in first dc to join.
Round 5: Change to yarn E. 1ch, 1dc in each st around, sl st in first dc to join.
Round 6: 3ch, 3tr in same st, miss 2 sts, 1dc in next st, *miss 2 sts, 7tr in next st, miss 2 sts, 1dc in next st; rep from * around, miss 2 sts, 3tr in same st as 3tr at beginning of round, sl st in third ch of beginning 3ch to join.
Round 7: Change to yarn A. 1ch, 1dc in first st, 2ch, tr7tog, *2ch, 1dc in fourth tr of 7tr from previous row, 2ch, tr7tog, 2ch; rep from * around, sl st in first dc to join.
Round 8: 1ch, *1dc in next st, miss 2 ch, 7tr in next st, miss 2 ch; rep from * around, sl st in first dc to join.
Round 9: Change to yarn B. 3ch, miss first dc, tr3tog, 2ch, 1dc in fourth tr of 7tr from previous round, *2ch, tr7tog, 2ch, 1dc in fourth tr of 7tr; rep from * to last 3 sts, 2ch, tr3tog inserting hook through centre of first tr3tog of round before final pull through to join.
Round 10: Rep Round 6.
Round 11: Change to yarn C and rep Round 7.
Round 12: Rep Round 8.
Round 13: Change to Yarn D and rep Round 9.
Round 14: Rep Round 6.

Round 15: Change to yarn E and rep Round 7.
Round 16: Rep Round 8.
Round 17: Change to yarn D and rep Round 9.
Round 18: 1ch, 1dc in each st around, working 1dc in each dc and top of each tr7tog, and 2dc in each ch-sp.
Round 19: Change to yarn C. 1ch, 1dc in each st around, sl st in first dc to join.
Round 20: Change to yarn B. 1ch, 1dc in each st around, sl st in first dc to join.
Round 21: Change to yarn A. 1ch, 1dc in each st around, sl st in first dc to join.
Round 22: Change to yarn E. 1ch, 1dc in each st around, sl st in first dc to join.
Round 23: 3ch, 1tr in each st around, sl st in third ch of 3ch to join.
Rounds 24–25: Continue with yarn E and rep Rounds 22–23. Fasten off.

Making Up and Finishing

Whip stitch (see page 118) the bottom edges of the bag together and weave in all loose ends.

To give the bottom a rounder shape, turn inside out, flatten the corners and fold so that roughly 3cm (1¼in) of corner is lying up against the bottom of the bag. Stitch in place.

Gently steam block into shape.

This was originally made as a crochet, knitting and general craft bag, but it works equally well as a big Mary Poppins-style holdall. The bow pocket at the front is ideal for keeping tools and everyday essentials close at hand.

craft carrier

Yarn

King Cole Big Value (super chunky weight; 100% acrylic; 81m/88yds per 100g/3½oz ball)

4 balls of 016 Heather (A)

Small quantity of DK weight yarn in Cream (B)

Hooks and Notions

8mm (US L/11) crochet hook

4mm (US G/6) crochet hook

Tapestry needle

Lining fabric: Two pieces measuring approx. 20cm x 35cm (7¾in x 13¾in), two pieces measuring 13cm x 20cm (5in x 7¾in) and one piece measuring 13cm x 35cm (5in x 13¾in)

13cm x 35cm (5in x 13¾in) piece of stiff interfacing to line the bottom of the bag

Sewing needle and matching thread

Tension

10 sts and 12 rows to 10cm (4in) measured over double crochet

Finished Size

38cm (15in) wide x 22cm (8¾in) long x 15cm (6in) deep excluding handles

18cm (7in) handle drop

Abbreviations

See page 125.

Pattern Notes

This bag benefits from having a lining, especially the stiff interfacing in the bottom to help it retain its shape.

For the Bag

Using yarn A and 8mm (US L/11) hook, make 35ch.

Row 1: 1dc in second ch from hook (missed ch does not count as st), 1dc in each ch to end, turn. *(34 sts)*

Rows 2–68: 1ch (does not count as st throughout), 1dc in each st to end, turn.

Fasten off.

For the Sides (make 2 alike)

Using yarn A and 8mm (US L/11) hook, make 13ch.

Row 1: 1dc in second ch from hook (missed ch does not count as st), 1dc in each ch to end, turn. *(12 sts)*

Rows 2–26: 1ch (does not count as st throughout), 1dc in each st, turn.

Fasten off.

TIP Using DK weight yarn to edge a super chunky yarn gives the overall finish a much daintier and more refined look.

For the Handles (make 2 alike)

Using yarn A and 8mm (US L/11) hook, make 36ch.

Row 1: 1dc in second ch from hook (missed ch does not count as st), 1dc in each ch to end, turn. *(35 sts)*

Rows 2–3: 1ch (does not count as st throughout), 1dc in each st, turn.

Fasten off and weave in ends.

Fold each handle in half lengthways and using yarn B and 4mm (US G/6) hook, miss the first few sts then work 2dc between each st to join the edges together, leaving a few sts open at the end. Fasten off.

For the Bow

Using yarn A and 8mm (US L/11) hook, make 27ch.

Row 1: 1tr in fourth ch from hook (missed ch count as 1tr), 1tr in each st to end, turn. *(25 sts)*

Rows 2–6: 3ch (counts as 1tr throughout), 1tr in each st to end, turn.

Fasten off and weave in ends.

Using yarn B and 4mm (US G/6) hook, work 2dc between each st around the entire edge of the piece and working 5dc into each corner. Fasten off.

Take a length of yarn B and bind around the middle of the piece to make a bow.

Making Up and Finishing

Line up the edge of one of the sides with one edge of the main body of the bag. Stitch together taking care to only stitch 26 rows of the main body to the 26 rows of the side-piece. Now stitch a further 16 rows from the main body along the bottom edge of the side-piece, then stitch the last 26 rows of the main body, up the other edge of the side-piece. Repeat for opposite end of the bag.

Using yarn B and 4mm (US G/6) hook, join yarn between any yarn A stitch on the top edge and work 2dc in each st around. Fasten off.

Sew the bow to the front, leaving the top parts open to form a pocket, and attach handles.

Weave in loose ends and gently steam block.

Sew together the lining pieces. Place the stiff interfacing in the bottom and hand sew the lining into place.

I was born at the very beginning of the 1980s and for me this clutch handbag epitomizes all of the things that were cool at that time – lightning strikes, gold, glitz and glam pirates. I love it!

retro clutch

Yarn

Lion Brand Wool-Ease (Aran weight; 78% acrylic, 19% wool, 3% polyester; 146m/160yds per 70g/2½oz ball)

   1 ball of 620-301 White (A)

Hayfield Bonus DK (DK weight;100% acrylic, 280m/306yds per 100g/3½oz ball)

   Small quantity of 992 Pink (B)
   Small quantity of 887 Bright Pink (C)
   Small quantity of 957 Primrose (D)

Hooks and Notions

4.5mm (US 7) crochet hook

Tapestry needle

Approx. 23cm x 26.5cm (9in x 10½in) piece of lining fabric

106cm (41½in) length of chain for the strap

2 buttons, approx. 1cm (½in) wide

Sewing needle and matching thread

Tension

18 sts and 20 rows to 10cm (4in) measured over waffle pattern

Finished Size

22cm (8½in) wide x 11cm (4½in) deep

Abbreviations

See page 125.

Pattern Notes

This clutch bag uses a waffle stitch pattern where you work between the chain-spaces (see page 110) from the previous row. It produces an ideal texture for weaving yarns into the surface to create a pattern or design.

For the Clutch

Using yarn A and 4.5mm (US 7) hook, make 45ch.

Row 1: 1dc in second ch from hook (missed ch does not count as st), *1ch, miss next ch, 1dc in next ch; rep from * to last ch, 1dc in last ch, turn.

Rows 2–52: 1ch (does not count as st throughout), 1dc in first st, *1ch, miss 1 st, 1dc in ch-sp; rep from * to last st, 1dc in last st, turn.

Row 53 (Buttonholes): 1ch, 1dc in first st, [1ch, miss 1 st, 1dc in ch-sp] twice, 3ch, miss 3 sts, 1dc in ch-sp, [1ch, miss 1 st, 1dc in ch-sp] 14 times, 3ch, miss 3 sts, 1dc in ch-sp, 1ch, miss 1 st, 1dc in each of last 2 sts, turn.

Row 54: Rep Row 2 working [1dc, 1ch, 1dc] around each 3ch from previous row. Fasten off.

Making Up and Finishing

Weave in loose ends and block.

Fold over 10.5cm (4in) of the clutch panel (ensure it's not the end with the buttonholes in), and using yarn A, whip stitch (see page 118) the sides together.

Using contrast yarns B, C, and D, whip stitch around the dc posts to make a lightning strike design.

Hem both short ends of the lining fabric. With right-sides together, fold over approx. 9cm (3½in) of the fabric and sew the side seams. Insert into the clutch, and hand-sew to the top edge of the bag. Fold under the raw edges of the bag flap lining and pin into place. Take care to ensure the buttonholes are not covered, and hand sew the lining in place.

Add the buttons and use a few stitches of yarn to secure the chain strap on either side.

TIP When embroidering, use the same colour in different tones next to one another to add a feeling of depth to the design.

TIP The strap can completely change the look of a bag. Try out different materials such as ribbons, chains or webbing to see what you prefer.

I saw a similar design for this bag, crafted in leather, while browsing a magazine and immediately fell in love with it. Being a lady of modest means, I knew the only way I was likely to get one was by making it myself. Crochet is such a great medium for this – working in the round, using a slightly smaller hook than the manufacturer suggests, you can create a perfect circle in a neat and tight material. I also got to add a stalk and leaf along with choosing my own super retro strap.

peachy

Yarn

Cascade Pacific (Aran weight; 60% acrylic, 40% merino wool; 195m/213yds per 100g/ 3½oz skein)

    1 skein of 017 Peach (A)
    1 skein of 052 Geranium (B)
Small quantity of DK weight yarns in green and brown

Hooks and Notions

4mm (US G/6) crochet hook

3.5mm (US E/4) crochet hook

Tapestry needle

20cm (8in) zip

115cm (45in) length of gold chain

2 D-rings

Sewing needle and matching thread

Brown sewing thread

Tension

20 sts and 22 rows to 10cm (4in) measured over double crochet

Finished Size

18cm (7in) diameter x 4cm (1½in) deep

Abbreviations

See page 125.

Pattern Notes

If you prefer the look of a solid all-over colour, omit yarn B and work two identical front panels.

For the Front Panel

Using yarn A and 4mm (US G/6) hook, make a magic ring.

Round 1: 1ch (does not count as st throughout), 6dc into the ring, sl st in first dc to join. *(6 sts)*

Round 2: 1ch, 2dc in each st around, sl st in first dc to join. *(12 sts)*

Round 3: 1ch, *2dc in first st, 1dc in next st; rep from * to end, sl st in first dc to join. *(18 sts)*

Round 4: 1ch, *2dc in first st, 1dc in next 2 sts; rep from * to end, sl st in first dc to join. *(24 sts)*

Round 5: 1ch, *2dc in first st, 1dc in next 3 sts; rep from * to end, sl st in first dc to join. *(30 sts)*

Round 6: 1ch, *2dc in first st, 1dc in next 4 sts; rep from * to end, sl st in first dc to join. *(36 sts)*

Round 7: 1ch, *2dc in first st, 1dc in next 5 sts; rep from * to end, sl st in first dc to join. *(42 sts)*

Round 8: 1ch, *2dc in first st, 1dc in next 6 sts; rep from * to end, sl st in first dc to join. *(48 sts)*

Round 9: 1ch, *2dc in first st, 1dc in next 7 sts; rep from * to end, sl st in first dc to join. *(54 sts)*

Round 10: 1ch, *2dc in first st, 1dc in next 8 sts; rep from * to end, sl st in first dc to join. *(60 sts)*

Round 11: 1ch, *2dc in first st, 1dc in next 9 sts; rep from * to end, sl st in first dc to join. *(66 sts)*

Round 12: 1ch, *2dc in first st, 1dc in next 10 sts; rep from * to end, sl st in first dc to join. *(72 sts)*

Round 13: 1ch, *2dc in first st, 1dc in next 11 sts; rep from * to end, sl st in first dc to join. *(78 sts)*

Round 14: 1ch, *2dc in first st, 1dc in next 12 sts; rep from * to end, sl st in first dc to join. *(84 sts)*

Round 15: 1ch, *2dc in first st, 1dc in next 13 sts; rep from * to end, sl st in first dc to join. *(90 sts)*

Round 16: 1ch, *2dc in first st, 1dc in next 14 sts; rep from * to end, sl st in first dc to join. *(96 sts)*

Fasten off.

For the Back Panel

Using yarn A and 4mm (US G/6) hook, make a magic ring.

Round 1: 1ch (does not count as st throughout), 6dc into the ring, sl st in first dc to join. *(6 sts)*

Round 2: 1ch, 2dc in each st around, sl st in first dc to join. *(12 sts)*

Round 3: 1ch, *2dc in first st, 1dc in next st; rep from * to end, sl st in first dc to join. *(18 sts)*

Commence Tapestry Crochet pattern (see page 122): For the following rounds, work in dc changing colour as indicated and working the stitches over the unused yarn as you go.

Round 4: Using yarn B, work 1ch, 2dc in first st, using yarn A, 1dc in next 2 sts, *2dc in next st, 1dc in next 2 sts; rep from * to end, sl st in first dc to join. *(24 sts)*

Round 5: Using yarn B, work 1ch, 2dc in first st, 1dc in next 3 sts, using yarn A, 2dc in next st, 1dc in next 2 sts, using yarn B, 1dc in next st, using yarn A, 2dc in next st, using yarn B, 1dc in next st, using yarn A 1dc in next 2 sts, *2dc in next st, 1dc in next 3 sts; rep from * to end, sl st in first dc to join. *(30 sts)*

Round 6: Using yarn A, 1ch, 2dc in first st, 1dc in next 2 sts, using yarn B, 1dc in next 2 sts, [2dc in next st, 1dc in next 4 sts] twice, using yarn A, *2dc in next st, 1dc in next 4 sts; rep from * to end, sl st in first dc to join. *(36 sts)*

Round 7: Using yarn B, work 1ch, [2dc in the first st, dc in the next 5 sts] 3 times, 2dc in next st, 1dc in next 2 sts, using yarn A, 1dc in next 3 sts, 2dc in next st, 1dc in next 5 sts, 2dc in next st, 1dc in next 3 sts, using yarn B, 1dc in last 2 sts, sl st in first dc to join. *(42 sts)*

Round 8: Using yarn B, work 1ch, [2dc in the first st, dc in the next 6 sts] 3 times, 2dc in next st, 1dc in next st, using yarn A, 1dc in next 5 sts, 2dc in next st, 1dc in next 6 sts, 2dc in next st, 1dc in next 2 sts, using yarn B, 1dc in last 4 sts, sl st in first dc to join. *(48 sts)*

Round 9: Using yarn B, work 1ch, [2dc in first st, 1dc in next 7 sts] 3 times, using yarn A, *2dc in next st, 1dc in next 7 sts; rep from * to end, sl st in first dc to join. *(54 sts)*

Round 10: Using yarn B, work 1ch, 2dc in first st, using yarn A, 1dc in next st, using yarn B, 1dc in next 7 sts, [2dc in next st, 1dc in next 8 sts] 3 times, 2dc in next st, 1dc in next 3 sts, using yarn A, 1dc in next 5 sts, 2dc in next st, 1dc in next 4 sts, using yarn B, 1dc in last 4 sts, sl st in first dc to join. *(60 sts)*

Round 11: Using yarn B, work 1ch, [2dc in first st, 1dc in next 9 sts] 3 times, using yarn A, 2dc in next st, using yarn B, 1dc in next 2 sts, using yarn A, 1dc in next 7 sts, *2dc in next st, 1dc in next 9 sts; rep from * to end, sl st in first dc to join. *(66 sts)*

Round 12: Using yarn B, work 1ch, [2dc in first st, 1dc in next 10 sts] 3 times, using yarn A, [2dc in first st, 1dc in next 10 sts] twice, 2dc in next st, 1dc in next 7 sts, using yarn B, 1dc in next 3 sts, sl st in first dc to join. *(72 sts)*

Round 13: Using yarn A, work 1ch, 2dc in first st, using yarn B, 1dc in next 11 sts, [2dc in the first st, dc in the next 11 sts] twice, 2dc in next st, 1dc in next 8 sts, using yarn A, 1dc in next st, using yarn B, 1dc in next 2 sts, 2dc in next st, using yarn A, 1dc in next 11 sts, 2dc in next st, 1dc in next 9 sts, using yarn B, 1dc in last 2 sts, sl st in first dc to join. *(78 sts)*

Round 14: Using yarn B, work 1ch, [2dc in the first st, 1dc in next 12 sts] 3 times, 2dc in next st, using yarn A, 1dc in next 12 sts, *2dc in first st, 1dc in next 12 sts; rep from * to end, sl st in first dc to join. *(84 sts)*

Round 15: Using yarn B, work 1ch, [2dc in first st, 1dc in next 13 sts] 3 times, using yarn A, *2dc in next st, 1dc in next 13 sts; rep from * to end, sl st in first dc to join. *(90 sts)*

Round 16: Using yarn B, work 1ch, [2dc in first st, 1dc in next 14 sts] 3 times, using yarn A, *2dc in first st, 1dc in next 14 sts; rep from * to end, sl st in first dc to join. *(96 sts)*

Fasten off.

For the Gusset

Using yarn A and 4mm (US G/6) hook, make 97ch.

Row 1: 1dc in second ch from hook (missed ch does not count as st), 1dc in each ch to end, turn. *(96 sts)*

Rows 2–4: 1ch (does not count as st throughout), 1dc in each st to end, turn.

Row 5: 1ch, 1dc in first 34 sts, make 38ch, miss 36 sts, 1dc in each of last 26 sts, turn.

Row 6: 1ch, 1dc in first 26 sts, work 36dc around ch, 1dc in each of last 34 sts, turn.

Rows 7-8: 1ch, 1dc in each st to end.

Fasten off.

For the Leaf

Using a small quantity of green yarn and 3.5mm (US E/4) hook, make 10ch. Sl st in first ch from hook, 1dc in next ch, 1htr in next ch, 1tr in next 2 ch, 1dtr in each of next 2 ch, 1tr in next 2 ch, 4tr in end ch, then working up the opposite side of chain, 1tr in next 2 ch, 1dtr in each of next 2 ch, 1tr in next 2 ch, 1htr in next ch, 1dc in next ch, sl st in end ch. Fasten off.

For the Stalk

Using a small quantity of brown yarn and 3.5mm (US E/4) hook, make 6ch. 1dc in second ch from hook, 1dc in each ch to end. Fasten off.

Making Up and Finishing

Weave in ends and block pieces to shape.

Lay the gusset piece flat. Place the zip so it fits neatly in the missed stitch gap and sew into place. Tack the ends of the zip to secure them.

Sew the short ends of the gusset together and sew to the front and back pieces using whip stitch (see page 118).

Sew the leaf and stalk into place.

Using a small amount of yarn A, attach D-rings to either side of the bag and then attach the chain strap.

I love bright colours and bold designs, and couldn't have made a collection without having one pattern influenced by the Mexican Day of the Dead festival. This super kitsch, super cool bag is brought alive with appliqué roses and a gold rope handle finished off with a fabulous, matching lining.

candy skull bag

Yarn

Cascade 220 (Aran weight; 100% Peruvian Highland wool; 200m/220yds per 100g/ 3½oz skein)

- 1 skein of 9478 Cotton Candy (A)
- 1 skein of 8687 Butter (B)
- 1 skein of 7814 Chartreuse (C)
- 1 skein of 8906 Blue Topaz (D)
- 1 skein of 9615 Bright Nectarine (E)
- 1 skein of 8505 White (F)
- 1 skein of 8555 Black (G)

Hooks and Notions

5mm (US H/8) crochet hook

4mm (US G/6) crochet hook

Tapestry needle

Approx. 19 x 51cm (7½in x 20in) piece of lining fabric (optional)

1m (1yd) length of 1cm (⅜in) diameter gold cord

Small quantity of gold embroidery thread

Tension

18 sts and 17 rows to 10cm (4in) measured over double crochet

Finished Size

18cm (7in) x 25cm (9¾in)

Abbreviations

See page 125.

For the Tote

Using yarn A and 5mm (US H/8) hook, make 33ch.

Row 1: 1dc in second ch from hook (missed ch does not count as st), 1dc in each st to end, turn. *(32 sts)*

Row 2: Change to yarn D. 1ch (does not count as st throughout), 1dc in each st to end, turn.

Row 3: Change to yarn C. 1ch, 1dc in each st to end, turn.

Row 4: Change to yarn B. 1ch, 1dc in each st to end, turn.

Row 5: Change to yarn E. 1ch, 1dc in each st to end, turn.

Row 6: Change to yarn A. 1ch, 1dc in each st to end, turn.

Rows 7–41: Rep Rows 2–6.

Rows 42–43: Continuing with yarn A. 1ch, 1dc in each st to end, turn.

Row 44: Change to yarn B. 1ch, 1dc in each st to end, turn.

Row 45: Change to yarn C. 1ch, 1dc in each st to end, turn.

Rows 46–50: Change to yarn D. 1ch, 1dc in each st to end, turn.

Commence Tapestry Crochet pattern (see page 122) and work in dc changing colour as indicated and working stitches over the unused yarn as you go. The number indicates the amount of stitches and the letter denotes the yarn colour. For example; 5A, 4B, 5A means work 5dc in A, 4dc in B, 5dc in A. See Chart for reference.

Row 1: 10D, 12B, 10D.
Row 2: 9D, 2B, 10E, 2B, 9D.
Row 3: 8D, 2B, 12E, 2B, 8D.
Row 4: 7D, 2B, 3E, 8F, 3E, 2B, 7D.
Row 5: 6D, 2B, 3E, 10F, 3E, 2B, 6D.
Row 6: 5D, 2B, 4E, 10F, 4E, 2B, 5D.
Row 7: 4D, 2B, 5E, 10F, 5E, 2B, 4D.
Row 8: 3D, 2B, 6E, 10F, 6E, 2B, 3D.
Row 9: 3D, 2B, 6E, 10F, 6E, 2B, 3D.
Row 10: 3D, 2B, 3E, 16F, 3E, 2B, 3D.
Row 11: 3D, 2B, 3E, 16F, 3E, 2B, 3D.
Row 12: 3D, 2B, 2E, 18F, 2E, 2B, 3D.
Row 13: 3D, 2B, 2E, 3F, 5G, 2F, 5G, 3F, 2E, 2B, 3D.
Row 14: 3D, 2B, 2E, 3F, 5G, 2F, 5G, 3F, 2E, 2B, 3D.
Row 15: 3D, 2B, 2E, 4F, 3G, 4F, 3G, 4F, 2E, 2B, 3D.
Row 16: 3D, 2B, 2E, 18F, 2E, 2B, 3D.

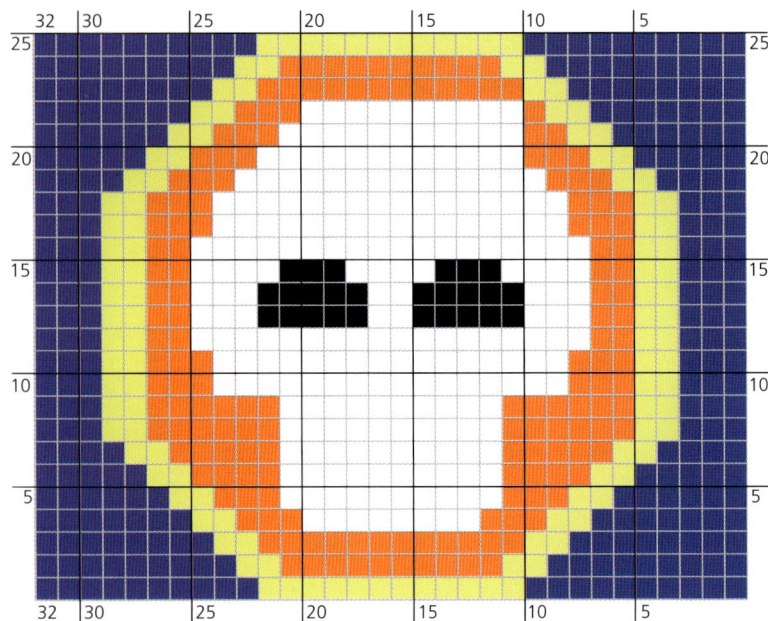

Key to chart

- Butter (B)
- Blue Topaz (D)
- Bright Nectarine (E)
- White (F)
- Black (G)

Row 17: 3D, 2B, 3E, 16F, 3E, 2B, 3D.

Row 18: 3D, 2B, 3E, 16F, 3E, 2B, 3D.

Row 19: 4D, 2B, 3E, 14F, 3E, 2B, 4D.

Row 20: 5D, 2B, 3E, 12F, 3E, 2B, 5D.

Row 21: 6D, 2B, 3E, 10F, 3E, 2B, 6D.

Row 22: 7D, 2B, 3E, 8F, 3E, 2B, 7D.

Row 23: 8D, 2B, 12E, 2B, 8D.

Row 24: 9D, 2B, 10E, 2B, 9D.

Row 25: 10D, 12B, 10D.

Now continue as follows:

Next 5 rows: Change to yarn D. 1ch, 1dc in each st to end, turn.

Next row: Change to yarn C. 1ch, 1dc in each st to end, turn.

Next row: Change to yarn B. 1ch, 1dc in each st to end, turn.

Next row: Change to yarn A. 1ch, 1dc in each st to end, turn. Fasten off.

For the Roses (make 5 alike)

Using yarn A and 4mm (US G/6) hook, make 37ch. Miss 2 ch, *5dc in next ch, miss 1ch; rep from * to end. Fasten off, leaving a long tail.

Thread the long tail through a tapestry needle, curl the strip into a rose shape and secure with a few stitches.

For the Leaves (make 5 alike)

Using yarn C and 4mm (US G/6) hook, make 4ch, sl st in first ch, 1dc in next ch, 1htr in next ch, 3htr in end ch. Working up the other side of the ch, 1htr in next ch, 1dc in next ch, sl st in last ch. Fasten off leaving a long tail.

Making Up and Finishing

Weave in ends on the tote panel and block to measurements.

Using a length of yarn G, thread the tapestry needle and backstitch (see page 124) around the edge of the skull and eye sockets. Using backstitch and chain stitch (see page 124), add nostrils, teeth, a few flowers, vines, and stars to the skull, using the photograph for reference.

Using the gold embroidery thread, backstitch around the outer edge of the yarn B circle framing the skull.

Sew the roses and leaves in place around the skull.

Attach the strap as follows: With a small amount of yarn A, bind the ends of the gold cord to prevent it from fraying. Hold one bound end at the bottom of one side of the bag, stitch it into the seam space, using a needle and the gold embroidery thread. Repeat from the bottom of the other side of the bag, leaving a long loop of the gold cord to form the strap.

Sew the sides of the lining fabric together and square off the bottom corners. Hem the top edge and hand sew the lining into the bag.

TIP This bag doesn't need any fancy embroidery stitches to be effective – a simple backstitch can be enough to give a really striking effect.

This rose design actually started as an image I was planning to paint on a wall, but once I'd charted it out I couldn't help myself from turning it into something I could carry around with me. The cross-stitched rose pattern and colours give this handbag a flavour of Eastern European folk art, and it's a genuine delight to have it close at hand.

rose handbag

Skill Level ★ ★ ☆

Yarn

Cascade 220 (Aran weight; 100% Peruvian Highland wool; 200m/220yds per 100g/3½oz skein)

1 skein of 8505 White (A)
Small quantities of the following shades:
7814 Chartreuse (B)
8114 Dusty Rose (C)
8267 Forest Green (D)
8415 Cranberry (E)
8913 Cherry Blossom (F)
8414 Bright Red (G)
8021 Beige (H)

Hooks and Notions

4mm (US G/6) crochet hook

Tapestry needle

2 bag handles or belts, 38cm (15in) length

Approx. 31cm x 47cm (12¼in x 18½in) piece of lining fabric

Sewing needle and matching thread

Tension

18 sts and 21 rows to 10cm (4in) measured over double crochet

Finished Size

30cm (11¾in) x 23cm (9in)

Abbreviations

See page 125.

Pattern Notes

The cross stitch rose design is embroidered into the grid formed in the bag panel by the natural spaces between each double crochet stitch.

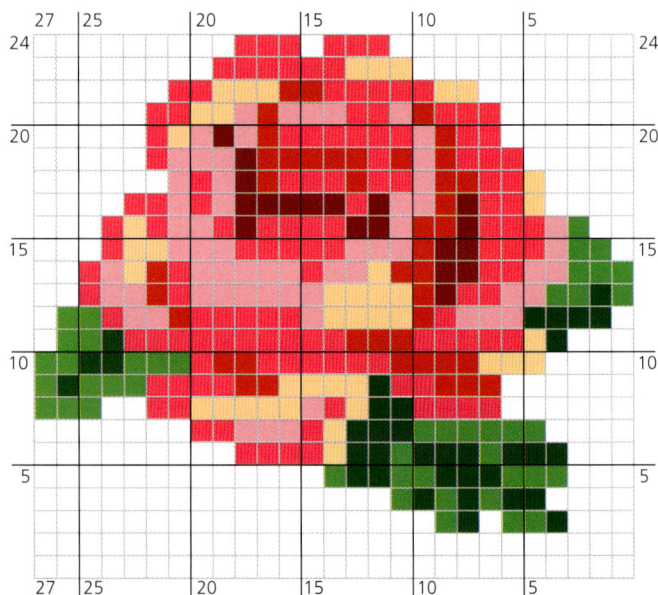

Key

- ☐ White (A)
- ■ Chartreuse (B)
- ■ Dusty Rose (C)
- ■ Forest Green (D)
- ■ Cranberry (E)
- ■ Cherry Blossom (F)
- ■ Bright Red (G)
- ■ Beige (H)

For the Panels (make 2 alike)

Using yarn A and 4mm (US G/6) hook, make 49ch.

Row 1: 1dc in second ch from hook (missed ch does not count as st), 1dc in each ch to end, turn. *(48 sts)*

Rows 2–43: 1ch (does not count as st throughout), 1dc in each st to end, turn.

Fasten off.

With RS facing, join yarn B in top left corner and work around three sides of the panel as follows:

Row 44: 1ch, 1dc between each row end to corner, 3dc in corner st, 1dc in each st along the bottom edge to corner, 3dc in corner, 1dc between each row end to corner, turn.

Row 45: Change to yarn C. 1ch, 1dc in each st to end, turn.

Row 46: Change to yarn F. 1ch, 1dc in each st to end, turn.

Row 47: Change to yarn E. 1ch, 1dc in each st to end, turn.

Row 48: Change to yarn D. 1ch, 1dc in each st to end, turn.

Fasten off.

Making Up and Finishing

Weave in loose ends and block to measurements.

Reading from the chart, cross-stitch (see page 124) the rose design on to one of the bag panels – pick a corner to start from, and work the cross-stitch pattern from there.

Thread a tapestry needle with a length of yarn D and whip stitch (see page 118) the front and back panels together along sides and bottom edge.

Attach the handles to the top of the bag.

Sew the sides of the lining fabric together and square off the bottom corners. Hem the top edge and hand sew the lining into the bag.

This super cute kitty would be ideal as a handbag for a small person, or a purse for a bigger person – by which I mean my 26-year-old sister!

little kitty handbag

Yarn

Cascade Pacific (Aran weight; 60% cotton, 40% Merino wool, 195m/213yds per 100g/3½oz ball)

1 ball of 02 White (A)
1 ball of 52 Geranium (B)

Hooks and Notions

4mm (US G/6) crochet hook

Locking stitch marker

Tapestry needle

1 button, 1cm (½in) diameter

Sewing needle and matching threads

1.25m (1¼yds) of bright pink cord

2 D-rings, 1.5cm (⅝in) across

Small amount of green felt

2 black sequins, 1.5cm (⅝in) diameter

2 white sequins, 0.5cm (¼in) diameter

Tension

First 5 rounds of double crochet to measure 5cm (2in) in diameter after blocking

Finished Size

11cm (4½in) diameter

Abbreviations

See page 125.

Pattern Notes

This bag is worked in a continuous spiral – use a locking stitch marker to keep track of the start of a round, moving it up as you complete each one.

For the Bag Panel (make 2 alike)

Using yarn A and 4mm (US G/6) hook, make a magic ring.

Round 1: 6dc into the ring. *(6 sts)*
Round 2: 2dc in each st around. *(12 sts)*
Round 3: *2dc in first st, 1dc in next st; rep from * to end. *(18 sts)*
Round 4: *2dc in first st, 1dc in next 2 sts; rep from * to end. *(24 sts)*
Round 5: *2dc in first st, 1dc in next 3 sts; rep from * to end. *(30 sts)*
Round 6: *2dc in first st, 1dc in next 4 sts; rep from * to end. *(36 sts)*
Round 7: *2dc in first st, 1dc in next 5 sts; rep from * to end. *(42 sts)*
Round 8: *2dc in first st, 1dc in next 6 sts; rep from * to end. *(48 sts)*
Round 9: *2dc in first st, 1dc in next 7 sts; rep from * to end. *(54 sts)*
Round 10: *2dc in first st, 1dc in next 8 sts; rep from * to end. *(60 sts)*
Round 11: *2dc in first st, 1dc in next 9 sts; rep from * to end. *(66 sts)*
Round 12: 2ch, 1htr in next 5 sts, 1dc in next 10 sts, 1htr in next 5 sts. Fasten off.

TIP The little decorative additions added to the handbag really bring it to life. Experiment with different eye shapes or button noses to give your kitty character.

For the Outer Ears (make 2 alike)
Using yarn A and 4mm (US G/6) hook, make 4ch, sl st in first ch to form a ring.

Row 1: 1ch, [2dc, 2ch, 2dc] into ring, turn.

Row 2: 1ch, 1dc in next 2 sts, 2dc in ch-sp, 2ch, 2dc in ch-sp, 1dc in last 2 sts.

Row 3: 1ch, 1dc in next 4 sts, 2dc in ch-sp, 2ch, 2dc in ch-sp, 1dc in next 4 sts.

Row 4: 1ch, 1dc in next 6 sts, 2dc in ch-sp, 2ch, 2dc in ch-sp, 1dc in next 6 sts.

For the Inner Ears (make 2 alike)
Using yarn B and 4mm (US G/6) hook, work as Rows 1–3 of Outer Ears. Fasten off.
Sew to Outer Ears and attach to body of bag.

For the Nose
Make a small loop of yarn and attach to tip of nose flap, close lid, mark place for nose button, and then sew button in place.

For the Eyes (both alike)
Cut two pieces of felt in an oval shape and sew onto either side of the nose. Sew the small sequin to the large sequin then sew both in place on the green felt.

For the Strap
Using a length of yarn A, attach the D-rings to either side of the bag. Thread the cord through the D-rings and bind the ends together using yarn B.

Making Up and Finishing
Weave in loose ends and gently steam block, avoiding the sequins.

For the Nose Flap
Using yarn A and 4mm (US G/6) hook, make 2ch.

Row 1: 1dc in second ch from hook (missed ch does not count as st), turn. *(1 st)*

Row 2: 1ch (does not count as st throughout), 2dc in next st, turn. *(2 sts)*

Row 3: 1ch, 2dc in first st, 1dc in next st, turn. *(3 sts)*

Row 4: 1ch, 2dc in first st, 1dc in next 2 sts, turn. *(4 sts)*

Row 5: 1ch, 2dc in first st, 1dc in next 3 sts, turn. *(5 sts)*

Row 6: 1ch, 2dc in first st, 1dc in next 4 sts, turn. *(6 sts)*

Row 7: 1ch, 2dc in first st, 1dc in next 5 sts, turn. *(7 sts)*

Row 8: 1ch, 2dc in first st, 1dc in next 6 sts, turn. *(8 sts)*

Row 9: 1ch, 2dc in first st, 1dc in next 7 sts, turn. *(9 sts)*

Row 10: 1ch, 2dc in first st, 1dc in next 8 sts, turn. *(10 sts)*

Row 11: 1ch, 2dc in first st, 1dc in next 9 sts, turn. *(11 sts)*

Row 12: 1ch, 2dc in first st, 1dc in next 10 sts, turn. *(12 sts)*

Row 13: 1ch, 2dc in first st, 1dc in next 11 sts, turn. *(13 sts)*

Row 14: 1ch, 2dc in first st, 1dc in next 12 sts, turn. *(14 sts)*

Row 15: 1ch, 2dc in first st, 1dc in next 13 sts, turn. *(15 sts)*

Row 16: 1ch, 2dc in first st, 1dc in next 14 sts, turn. *(16 sts)*

Row 17: 1ch, 2dc in first st, 1dc in next 15 sts, turn. *(17 sts)*
Fasten off.
Sew the Nose Flap to Round 12 of one of the circular pieces. Sew the two circular panels together leaving an opening of 9cm (3½in).

These little bags were made at the request of my boys. The eldest has just joined the Scouts and wanted something to keep his essentials in that he could easily identify as his and which wouldn't get in the way. All of the colours are chosen by him and as soon as I'd made one, the littlest wanted one too; he may not be old enough to join the Scouts yet, but he'll be ready when he is! Pick your little Scout's initial from the charts overleaf and you can make one for them, too.

scout pocket bag

Skill Level ★ ★ ✲

Yarn

DMC Natura XL Just Cotton (super chunky weight; 100% cotton, 72m/82yds per 100g/3½oz ball)

- 1 ball of 08 dark green (A)
- 1 ball of 101 dark orange (B)
- 1 ball of 84 khaki (C)

Hooks and Notions

5mm (US H/8) crochet hook

Tapestry needle

Tension

11 sts and 12 rows to 10cm (4in) measured over tapestry double crochet

Finished Size

12cm (4¾in) x 13cm (5¼in)

Abbreviations

See page 125.

For the Bag

Using yarn A and 5mm (US H/8) hook, make 14ch.

Set-up row: 1dc in second ch from hook (missed ch does not count as st), 1dc in each ch to end, turn. *(13 sts)*

Rows 1–15: 1ch (does not count as stitch throughout), 1dc in each st across, turn.

Row 16: 1ch, 1dc in BLO of each st to end, turn.

Rows 17–31: Reading from the Chart of your choosing (see overleaf) and working 1ch before beginning each row, commence Tapestry Crochet pattern (see page 122) and work in dc changing colour as indicated and working stitches over the unused yarn as you go.

Fasten off.

Making Up and Finishing

Sew sides together.

Weave in loose ends and block.

Cut three equal lengths of yarn B. Tie them together at one end, plait the lengths together then tie a knot at the other end. Sew securely to the inside of the bag.

TIP Measure the height of your Scout before making the strap and adjust the length as necessary.

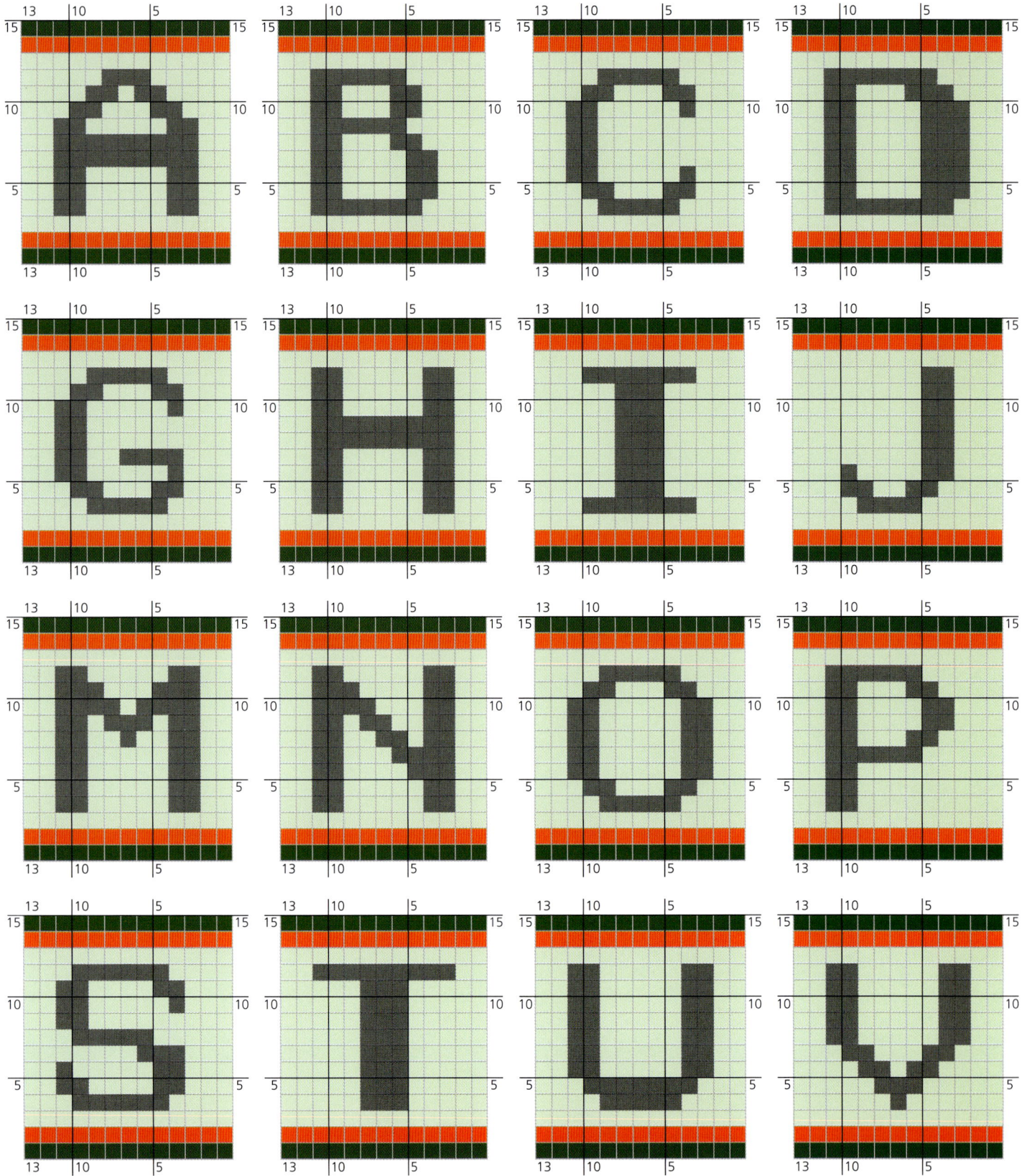

Key ▊ dark ▊ dark ▊ khaki (C)
green (A) orange (B)

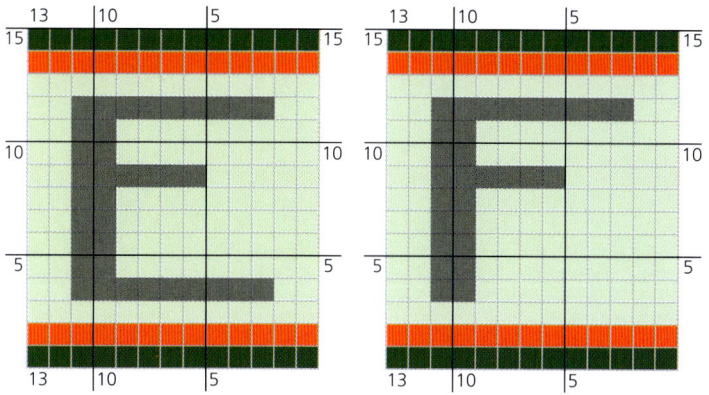

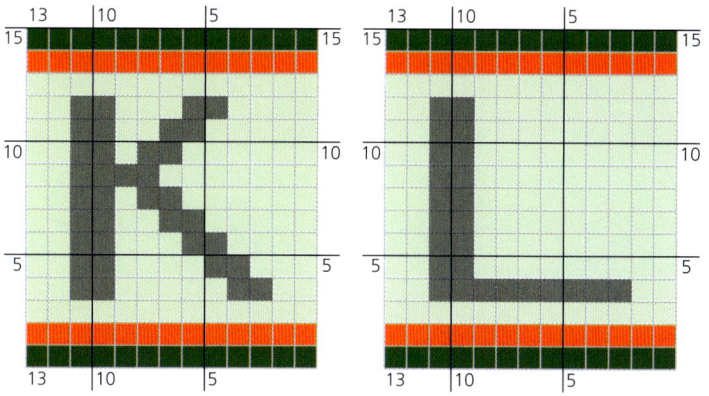

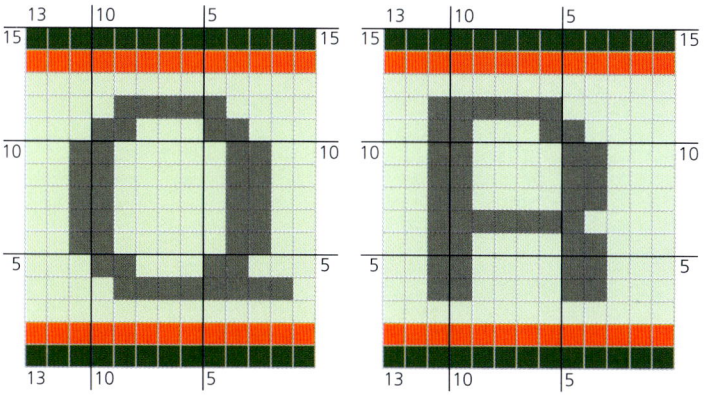

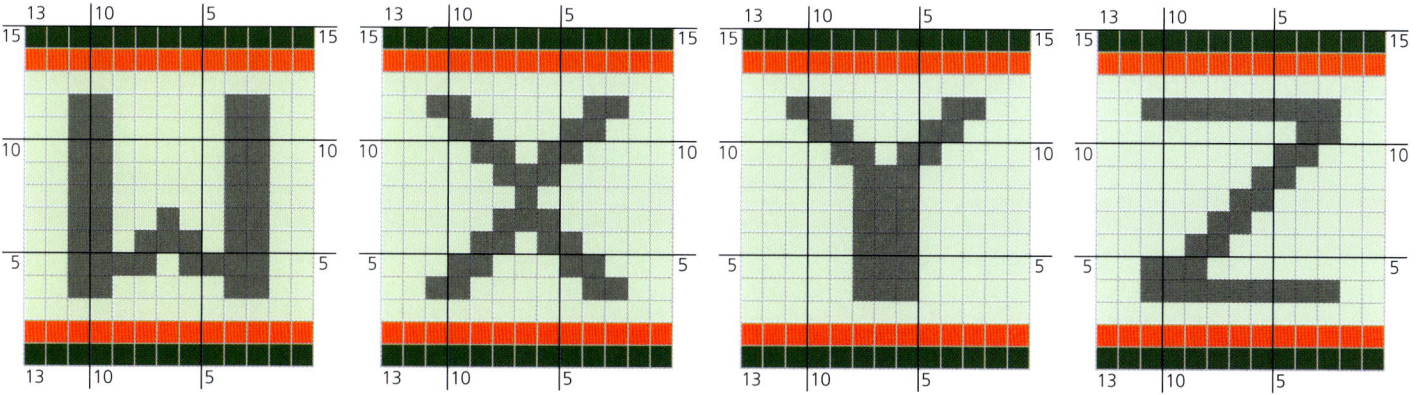

Originally this was going to be for my husband, a handy-sized boy's bag to throw his keys and phone in. But then I fell in love with the tweed yarn and the simple, classic elegance of it, so I added a little row of star stitches and it may only be subtle, but it's a little bit too feminine for him to use. If you are feeling generous and want to make this for your man, just leave out the little row of star stitches.

mini satchel

Skill Level ✱ ✱ ✱

Yarn

Berroco Meraki (DK weight; 71% cotton, 24% hemp, 5% polyester; 120m/131yd per 50g/1¾oz ball)

   3 balls of 6048 Relax

Small quantity of contrasting yarn for sewing

Hooks and Notions

4mm (US G/6) crochet hook

Tapestry needle

2 x 2cm (¾in) wide brown leather belts (if placing buckles on front as shown) or approx. 1m (1yd) long 2cm (¾in) wide brown leather strap (no front fastening)

Approx. 26 x 50cm (10¼in x 19¾in) piece of lining fabric

Awl

2 D-rings

Tension

18 sts and 16 rows to 10cm (4in) measured over half treble crochet BLO

Finished Size

20cm (8in) deep x 25cm (9¾in) wide

Abbreviations

See page 125.

Pattern notes

Working into htr through the back loop only (BLO – see page 114) gives the lovely stockinette stitch effect. The body of the satchel is worked in the round and the flap is then worked back and forth in rows. The first row is worked flat to make it easier to join in the round.

For the Bag

Using yarn A and 4mm (US G/6) hook, leaving a long tail, make 102ch.
Row 1: 1htr in third ch from hook (missed 2ch counts as st), 1htr in each ch to end, join in the round with a sl st in first htr. *(100 sts)*
Rounds 2–30: 2ch (counts as 1htr throughout), 1htr BLO in each st around, join with a sl st in top of 2ch.
Round 31: 1ch (does not count as st), 1dc BLO in each st around, join with a sl st in first dc.
Row 32: 2ch, 1htr in each of next 39 sts, turn. *(40 sts)*
Rows 33–45: Working back and forth on these 40 sts only, 2ch, 1htr **between** posts, turn.
Row 46 (star stitch): 3ch, pull up a loop in second ch from hook, pull up a loop in third ch from hook, pull up a loop in each of next 2 sts, yrh and pull through all 5 loops on hook, 1ch to close the star, *pull up a loop in centre of star last star made, pull up a loop around bottom left post/stitch of the star, pull up a loop in each of next 2 sts, yrh and pull through all 5 loops on hook, 1ch to close; rep from * to end, turn.
Row 47: 2ch, 2htr in centre of each star across.
Row 48: Sl st in each st across.
Fasten off.

Making Up and Finishing

Weave in all loose ends and steam block to measurements. Using whip stitch (see page 118), sew the bottom of the bag closed. To square off the corners, turn the satchel inside out, fold over each bottom corner approx. 3cm (1¼in) and tack the corner point to the bottom seam. Turn right side out again.

For the Straps

Using a length of the contrast yarn, thread the tapestry needle and attach a D-ring to either side of the bag. If using belts, cut the buckle off one end (leaving enough length to attach it to the bag as a fastening), and cut 12cm (4¾in) from the other end. Put these ends to one side. On the remaining long length of one of the belts, fold one end over approx. 4cm (1½in) and, using an awl (or a sharp tool), make a hole through the folded part and the belt. Thread it through the D-ring on one side of bag and, using a length of brightly coloured yarn, sew through the hole to secure in place. Repeat for other side.

For the Fastenings

Using the awl, make a hole in the bottom centre of each of the buckle ends, and then sew in place on your bag using a length of brightly coloured yarn, using the photos for reference. Make a similar hole in the remaining belt ends and sew them in place on the bag in line with the buckle ends (you may find it easier to buckle the ends together before sewing to make sure they are sewn down in the correct place).

For the Lining

Hem both short ends of the lining fabric. With right-sides together, fold over approx. 20cm (8in) of the fabric and sew the side seams. Insert into the bag, and hand-sew to the top edge of the bag. Fold under the raw edges of the lining for the bag flap, shaping the corners as necessary, and pin into place on the inside of the flap. Hand sew the lining in place.

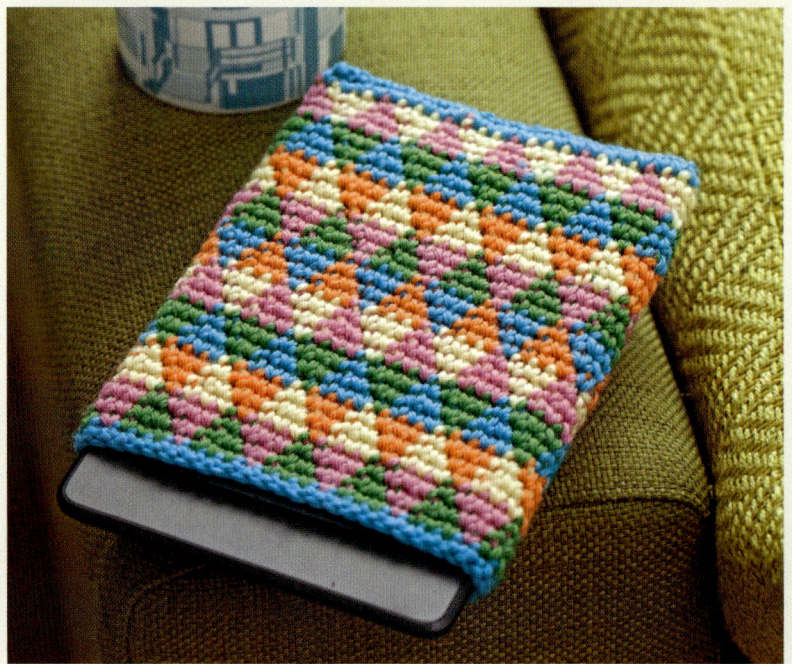

chapter 3 **in your bag**

This is the first piece of tapestry crochet I ever made, and it is a great piece to start with. The bold colours remind me of summer and the strong contrast between each one makes it clear when to change shades. This is a quick make, so play with the colours and make one to go with each bag or outfit!

zigzag glasses case

Yarn

Jarol Heritage DK (DK weight; 55% wool, 25% acrylic, 20% nylon; 250m/273yds per 100g/3½oz ball)

- 1 ball of 133 Cerise (A)
- 1 ball of 150 Spice (B)
- 1 ball of 140 Gold (C)
- 1 ball of 137 Lime (D)
- 1 ball of 100 Cream (E)

Hooks and Notions

4mm (US G/6) crochet hook

Locking stitch marker

Tapestry needle

Tension

22 sts and 21 rows to 10cm (4in) measured over double crochet

Finished Size

7.5cm (3in) x 19cm (7½in)

Abbreviations

See page 125.

Pattern Notes

The Chart is read from bottom to top and from right to left on every row. In order to keep the zigzags lined up you will need to shift the beginning of the round at Round 7 and all instructions on how to do this are given in the pattern.

The case is worked in a continuous spiral – use a locking stitch marker to keep track of the start of a round, moving it up as you complete each one.

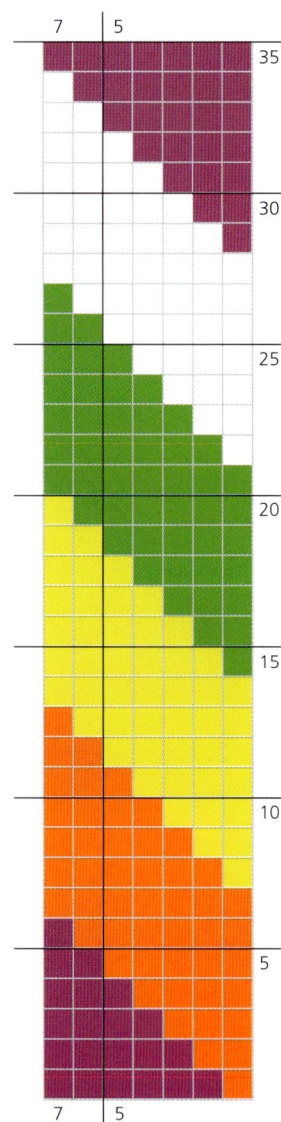

For the Case

Using yarn A and 4mm (US G/6) hook, make 17ch.

Set-up round: 2dc in second ch from hook (missed ch does not count as st), 1dc in next 14 ch, 3dc in end ch. Working up the other side of the ch, 1dc in next 14 ch, 2dc in last ch, sl st in first dc to join and place locking stitch marker to indicate beginning of round. *(35 sts)*

Commence Tapestry Crochet pattern (see page 122) and work in dc changing colour as indicated and working stitches over the unused yarn as you go. The number indicates the amount of stitches and the letter denotes the yarn colour. For example; 5A, 4B, 5A means work 5dc in A, 4dc in B, 5dc in A. The Chart may be used for reference, but please note the beginning of round shift that occurs in Round 7 as given below.

Round 1: *1B, 6A; rep from * to end.
Round 2: *2B, 5A; rep from * to end.
Round 3: *3B, 4A; rep from * to end.
Round 4: *4B, 3A; rep from * to end.
Round 5: *5B, 2A; rep from * to end.
Round 6: *6B, 1A; rep from * to end.

Key

- ▧ Cerise (A)
- ▨ Gold (C)
- ☐ Cream (E)
- ▧ Spice (B)
- ▨ Lime (D)

Round 7: Using yarn B only and working over yarn A to maintain even tension, 1dc in each st around. Remove locking stitch marker, work 1dc in each of next 3 sts, replace marker in next st to indicate new beginning of round. Fasten off yarn A.
Join yarn C and rep Rounds 1–7 working with yarns B and C.
Continue working reps of Rounds 1–7 changing colours as shown in the Chart.
Fasten off.

Making Up and Finishing
Weave in all loose ends and block to measurements.

TIPS
Working tapestry crochet in the round makes the design 'lean' to create a zigzag pattern.

As much as I like to think of myself as an elegant Scandi-style minimalist, I just can't help myself when it comes to sparkly things! On rare occasions when my husband and I do get away for a night, the sparkle and stars of this cosmetics purse make me feel super glam when I'm digging around for my liquid liner and red lipstick.

cosmetics purse

Yarn

Bergere de France Galaxie (super chunky weight; 80% acrylic, 18% wool, 2% polyester; 35m/38yds per 50g/1¾oz ball)

  1 ball of 251701 Sirius (A)
  2 balls of 25139 Aphelie (B)

Hooks and Notions

8mm (US L/11) crochet hook

Tapestry needle

Approx. 26.5cm x 47cm (10½in x 18½in) piece of lining fabric

20cm (8in) zip

Sewing needle and matching thread

Silver embroidery thread for securing the tassel

Tension

10 sts and 10 rows to 10cm (4in) measured over double crochet

Finished Size

25cm (10in) wide x 23cm (9in) deep

Abbreviations

See page 125.

For the Purse

Using yarn A and 8mm (US L/11) hook, make 22ch.

Round 1: 1dc in second ch from hook (missed ch does not count as st), 1dc in next 19 ch, 3dc in end ch. Working up the other side of the ch, 1dc in next 19 ch, 2dc in end ch, sl st in first dc to join. *(44 sts)*

Rounds 2–9: 1ch (does not count as st throughout), 1dc in each st around, sl st in first dc to join.

Round 10: Change to yarn B. 1ch, *[1dc, 1ch, 1dc] in next st, miss 1 st; rep from * to end, sl st in first dc to join.

Rounds 11–23: 1ch, [1dc, 1ch, 1dc] in each ch-sp to end, sl st in first dc to join.

Round 24: Change to yarn A. 1ch, *1dc in first 2 sts, miss 1 st; rep from * to end, sl st in first dc to join.

Fasten off.

Making Up and Finishing

Weave in all loose ends and gently block to measurements.

Sew the bottom edge closed. To square off the corners, turn the purse inside out, fold over each bottom corner approx. 3cm (1¼in) and tack the corner point to the bottom seam. Turn right side out again.

Sew the sides of the lining fabric together and square off the bottom corners. Hem the top edge and hand sew the lining into the purse. Insert the zip, hand-stitching it into place.

Fold several strands of yarn A to make a chunky tassel (see page 120). Wrap the silver embroidery thread around the folded end of the tassel, and use the thread to secure it to the zip-pull.

When my Grandpa proposed to my Grandma, they were in their early twenties, both were at university, neither had much to their name and, as he didn't have a ring to give her, he picked a forget-me-not and tied it around her finger. These cases were made for them, and the Loveheart one in particular is taken from the colours found in forget-me-nots.

spring glasses cases

Skill Level ✱ ✱ ✱

Yarn

Rico Essentials Cotton (DK weight; 100% cotton; 120m/131yd per 50g/1¾oz ball)

- 1 ball of 080 White (A)
- 1 ball of 073 Alga (B)
- 1 ball of 111 Violet (C)
- 1 ball of 033 Turquoise (D)

Hooks and Notions

4mm (US G/6) crochet hook

Locking stitch marker

Tapestry needle

Tension

22 sts and 21 rows to 10cm (4in) measured over tapestry double crochet

Finished Size

Striped Case: 7.5cm (3in) wide x 17cm (6¾in) long

Loveheart Case: 8cm (3¼in) wide x 17.5m (7in) long

Abbreviations

See page 125.

Pattern Notes

There are two different versions of this pattern; one in stripes and one with motifs and the possibilities for playing with colours are endless!

For the Striped Case

Using yarn A and 4mm (US G/6) hook, leaving a long tail, make 36ch. Taking care not to twist the ch, work a sl st in first ch to form a round.

Round 1: Work 1ch (does not count as st throughout), 1dc in each ch around, sl st in first dc to join. *(36 sts)*

Commence Tapestry Crochet pattern (see page 122) and work in dc changing colour as indicated and working stitches over the unused yarn as you go. The number indicates the amount of stitches and the letter denotes the yarn colour. For example; 5A, 4B, 5A means work 5dc in A, 4dc in B, 5dc in A.

Rounds 2–25: 1ch, *1A, 5B, 1A, 5C, 1A, 5D; rep from * around.

Leaving Yarn A attached, fasten off all other yarns.

Round 26: 1ch, 1dc in each st around.

Round 27: Sl st in each st around.

Fasten off.

For the Loveheart Case

Using yarn A and 4mm (US G/6) hook, leaving a long tail, make 35ch.

Row 1: 1dc in second ch from hook (missed ch does not count as st), 1dc in each st to end, turn. *(34 sts)*

Rows 2–3: 1ch (does not count as st throughout), 1dc in each st across, turn.

Commence Tapestry Crochet pattern (see page 122) and work in dc changing colour as indicated and working stitches over the unused yarn as you go. The number indicates the amount of stitches and the letter denotes the yarn colour. For example; 5A, 4B, 5A means work 5dc in A, 4dc in B, 5dc in A. See Chart for reference.

TIP The Striped Case is worked in the round as a spiral. You may find it helpful to mark the first stitch of the round with a locking stitch marker, moving it up as you complete each round.

Row 1: 1ch, 25A, 4D, 5A, turn.
Row 2: 1ch, 3A, 7D, 24A, turn.
Row 3: 1ch, 23A, 9D, 2A, turn.
Row 4: 1ch, 2A, 10D, 22A, turn.
Row 5: 1ch, 21A, 11D, 2A, turn.
Row 6: 1ch, 3A, 11D, 20A, turn.
Row 7: 1ch, 19A, 11D, 4A, turn.
Row 8: 1ch, 3A, 11D, 20A, turn.
Row 9: 1ch, 21A, 11D, 2A, turn.
Row 10: 1ch, 2A, 10D, 22A, turn.
Row 11: 1ch, 23A, 9D, 2A, turn.
Row 12: 1ch, 3A, 7D, 24A, turn.
Row 13: 1ch, 25A, 4D, 5A, turn.
Rows 14–15: 1ch, 34A, turn.
Row 16: 1ch, 25A, 4C, 5A, turn.
Row 17: 1ch, 3A, 7C, 24A, turn.
Row 18: 1ch, 23A, 9C, 2A, turn.
Row 19: 1ch, 2A, 10C, 22A, turn.
Row 20: 1ch, 21A, 11C, 2A, turn.
Row 21: 1ch, 3A, 11C, 20A, turn.
Row 22: 1ch, 19A, 11C, 4A, turn.
Row 23: 1ch, 3A, 11C, 20A, turn.
Row 24: 1ch, 21A, 11C, 2A, turn.
Row 25: 1ch, 2A, 10C, 22A, turn.
Row 26: 1ch, 23A, 9C, 2A, turn.
Row 27: 1ch, 3A, 7C, 24A, turn.
Row 28: 1ch, 25A, 4C, 5A, turn.
Rows 29–30: 1ch, 34A, turn.
Leaving yarn A attached, fasten off all other yarns.
Row 31: Sl st in each st across.
Fasten off.

Making Up and Finishing

Striped case only: Use the long tail to whip stitch (see page 118) the bottom edge of the case closed.

Loveheart case only: Fold in half lengthways and whip stitch the bottom and side edges closed.

Both cases: Weave in all loose ends and block to measurements.

Key

- ☐ White (A)
- ■ Violet (C)
- ■ Turquoise (D)

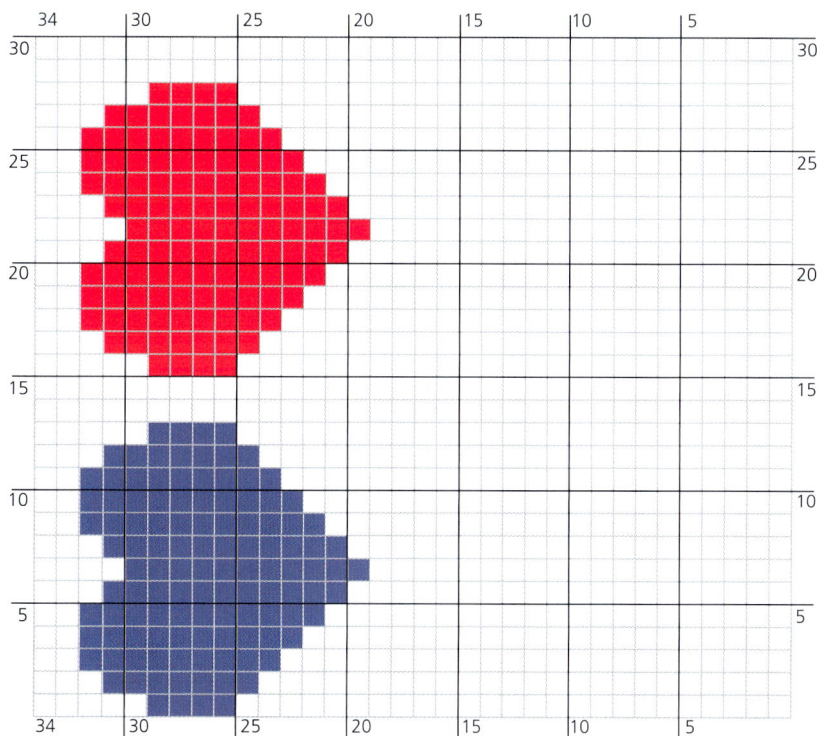

When I was 18, my then boyfriend (now husband) bought me a leather, strawberry shaped purse which I treasured and loved until it fell to pieces. 18 years on and I've made myself a new one in the most beautiful, hand-dyed yarn I could find, and I'll treasure it all over again.

strawberry purse

Yarn

Madelinetosh Unicorn Tails (4-ply weight; 100% superwash Merino wool; 48m/52yds per 15g/½oz skein)

 1 skein of Torchère

Hooks and Notions

2.75mm (US C/2) crochet hook

Tapestry needle

10cm (4in) red zip

Sewing needle

Red sewing thread

Green and white embroidery thread

Tension

First 8 rounds of double crochet to measure 5cm (2in) diameter

Finished Size

9cm (3½in) diameter

Abbreviations

See page 125.

Pattern Notes

This purse is worked in two pieces (front and back) before fitting the zip and sewing the seams together. I highly recommend taking time to block the front and back piece before seaming the sides in order to achieve a neater and more evenly finished purse. Block the two pieces on top of one another to ensure they are the same size and shape.

For the Purse (make 2 alike)

Using 2.75mm (US C/2) hook, make a magic ring.

Round 1: 1ch (does not count as st throughout), 6dc into the ring, sl st in first dc to join. *(6 sts)*

Round 2: 1ch, 2dc in each st around, sl st in first dc to join. *(12 sts)*

Round 3: 1ch, *2dc in next st, 1dc in next st; rep from * around, sl st in first dc to join. *(18 sts)*

Round 4: 1ch, *2dc in next st, 1dc in next 2 sts; rep from * around, sl st in first dc to join. *(24 sts)*

Round 5: 1ch, *2dc in next st, 1dc in next 3 sts; rep from * around, sl st in first dc to join. *(30 sts)*

Round 6: 1ch, *2dc in next st, 1dc in next 4 sts; rep from * around, sl st in first dc to join. *(36 sts)*

Round 7: 1ch, *2dc in next st, 1dc in next 5 sts; rep from * around, sl st in first dc to join. *(42 sts)*

Round 8: 1ch, *2dc in next st, 1dc in next 6 sts; rep from * around, sl st in first dc to join. *(48 sts)*

Round 9: 1ch, 1dc in first 2 sts, 1htr in next st, 2htr in each of next 4 sts, 1htr in next 3 sts, 1dc in next 10 sts, 1htr in next 3 sts, 3htr in next st, 1htr in next 3 sts, 1dc in next 10 sts, 1htr in next 3 sts, 2htr in each of next 4 sts, 1htr in next st, 1dc in next 3 sts, sl st in first dc to join. *(58 sts)*

Round 10: 1ch, 1dc in next 3 sts, [1htr in next st, 2htr in next st] 3 times, 1htr in next 2 sts, [2htr in next st, 1htr in next st] twice, 1htr in next st, 1dc in next 9 sts, 1htr in next 3 sts, 2htr in next st, 1htr in next 3 sts, 1dc in next 9 sts, 1htr in next st, [1htr in next st, 2htr in next st] twice, 1htr in next 2 sts, [2htr in next st, 1htr in next st] 3 times, 1dc in next 4 sts, sl st in first dc to join. *(69 sts)*

Round 11: 2ch (does not count as st), [1htr in first 10 sts, 2htr in next st] 3 times, 1htr in next st, work 3htr between 2htr of previous round, 1htr in next st, [2htr in next st, 1htr in next 10 sts] 3 times, 1htr in last st, sl st in first second ch of 2ch to join. *(78 sts)*

Fasten off.

Making Up and Finishing

Weave in loose ends and block the pieces.

Holding the Front and Back with WS together, taking the hook through both pieces, rejoin yarn at the top centre of the strawberry. Working through BLO of one piece and FLO of the other (see page 114), work 1htr in next 40 sts only – this will leave an opening down the side for the zip. Fasten off and weave in ends.

Using white embroidery thread, decorate the front with short, straight stitches for the strawberry seeds.

Sew the zip into the gap left in the side of the purse, then, using the green embroidery thread, add a few stitches to the top edge in the shape of leaves.

This is a great pattern for using up odds and ends of yarn left over from previous projects as you can put in as many retro racing stripes as you like. The design shown here was a request from my husband, who is a fan of all things 1980s, hence the primary colours. I've made myself one too, in mint green and pinks, and embellished it with cute buttons.

retro racer phone case

Yarn

Cascade 220 (Aran weight; 100% Peruvian Highland wool; 200m/220yds per 100g/3½oz skein)

- 1 skein of 9615 Bright Nectarine (A)
- 1 skein of 8687 Butter (B)
- 1 skein of 8895 Christmas Red (C)
- 1 skein of 8906 Blue Topaz (D)

Hooks and Notions

4mm (US G/6) crochet hook

Tapestry needle

Tension

18 sts and 20 rows to 10cm (4in) measured over double crochet

Finished Size

8.5cm (3¼in) wide x 15cm (6in) long

Abbreviations

See page 125.

Pattern Notes

This pattern can be adjusted to fit any phone or hand-held tablet. Simply take the width measurement and double it to calculate the length of the foundation chain, then work rounds to the desired length.

Cut and rejoin each yarn as you change colours (see page 117) and work over the ends as you go to save having to weave them all in at the end.

For the Case

Using yarn A and 4mm (US G/6) hook, make 33ch, sl st in first ch to form a ring, taking care not to twist the chain.

Rounds 1–4: 1ch (does not count as st throughout), 1dc in each st around, sl st in first dc to join. *(33 sts)*

Round 5: Using yarn B, 1ch, 1dc in first 11 sts, change to yarn A for last 22 sts, sl st in first dc to join.

Round 6: Using yarn C, 1ch, 1dc in first 10 sts, change to yarn B for last 23 sts, sl st in first dc to join.

Round 7: Using yarn D, 1ch, 1dc in first 9 sts, change to yarn C for last 24 sts, sl st in first dc to join.

Round 8: Using yarn A, 1ch, 1dc in first 8 sts, change to yarn D for last 25 sts, sl st in first dc to join.

Rounds 9–28: Using yarn A, 1ch, 1dc in each st around, sl st in first dc to join.

Fasten off.

Making Up and Finishing

Weave in all loose ends and whip stitch (see page 118) the bottom edges of the case together. Gently steam block to even out the stitches.

TIP Add as many retro racing stripes as you like and play around with colour – try brights, neutrals, create a series of gradient stripes, or simply use whatever is to hand in your oddments stash.

The colour palette for this sweet little wallet was inspired by a doughnut that I stole off my littlest monkey just so I could photograph it! He was most unhappy, but I was very pleased with the end result. Just the right size for keeping your credit and craft-shop loyalty cards safe, you literally don't need anything else than this in your pocket when you pop out in a yarn emergency.

corner-to-corner card wallet

Skill Level ✱ ✱ ✱

Yarn

DMC Natura Just Cotton (4-ply weight; 100% cotton; 155m/169yds per 50g/1¾oz ball)

1 ball of 62 Cerise (A)
1 ball of 47 Safran (B)
1 ball of 16 Tournesol (C)

Hooks and Notions

3.25mm (US D/3) crochet hook

Tapestry needle

10cm (4in) zip

Approx. 12in x 18cm (4¾in x 7in) piece of lining fabric

Sewing needle and matching thread

Tension

Finished piece (before making up) to measure 12cm (4¾in) wide x 16.5cm (6½in) long

Finished Size

11cm (4¼in) wide x 7.5cm (3in) deep

Abbreviations

See page 125.

Pattern Notes

'Corner-to-corner' crochet is worked in a diagonal direction from one corner, gradually increasing the number of 'blocks' to the required width, before decreasing up toward the opposite corner. It's a really fun stitch pattern and easy to get to grips with – this project is perfect for learning and practising the technique.

For the Case

Using yarn A and 3.25mm (US D/3) hook, make 6ch.

Row 1: 1tr in fourth ch from hook (missed 3ch counts as 1tr throughout), 1tr in each of next 2 ch, turn. *(1 block made)*

Row 2: Change to yarn B. Work 6ch, 1tr in fourth ch from hook, 1tr in each of next 2 ch. Turn block slightly so the side of this block lies along the top of the first block made in Row 1. Sl st in the top of 3ch from Row 1, work 3ch, then work 3tr around 3ch from Row 1. You should now have a small 'V' shape made of 3 blocks.

Row 3: Change to yarn C. Work 6ch, 1tr in fourth ch from hook, 1tr in each of next 2 ch. *Turn block slightly so the side of this block lies along the top of block made in previous row, sl st in the top of 3ch of block in previous row, work 3ch, then work 3tr around 3ch of block in previous row; repeat from * to end.

Rows 4–9: Rep Row 3, continuing to work stripes in yarns A, B, and C, until you have a piece of work that is 9 blocks across.

Row 10: Continuing to alternate yarns as set, turn your work, sl st in each of 3 tr just made, 3ch, work 3tr around 3ch of block in previous row, *sl st in the top of 3ch of next block in previous row, work 3ch, then work 3tr around 3ch of block in previous row; rep from * to end, turn.

Row 11: 6ch, 1tr in fourth ch from hook, 1tr in each of next 2 ch, *sl st in the top of 3ch of block in previous row, work 3ch, then work 3tr around 3ch of block in previous row; rep from * to last block of row, sl st in the top of 3ch of last block in previous row, turn.

Row 12: Rep Row 10.

Row 13: Rep Row 11.

Row 14: Sl st in each of 3 tr just made, 3ch, work 3tr around 3ch of block in previous row, *sl st in the top of 3ch of next block in previous row, work 3ch, then work 3tr around 3ch of block in previous row; rep from * to last block of row, sl st in the top of 3ch of last block in previous row, turn.

Rows 15–21: Rep Row 14 until 1 block remains.

Fasten off.

Making Up and Finishing

Weave in loose ends and gently block.

Fold the case panel in half so the short edges touch. Using a tapestry needle and length of yarn, sew each side together. Repeat with the piece of lining material, hem the top and tack inside the crochet case. Hand sew the zip in place.

As a crochet addict, I tend to take my hooks everywhere. This fantastic, foxy carry case has pockets for each of your favourite hooks as well as a bigger pocket for scissors, notions, and needles. This may well be the most used make in the entire collection!

foxy crochet carry case

Skill Level ✱ ✱ ✱

Yarn
DMC Natura XL Just Cotton (super chunky weight; 100% cotton, 82m/75m per 100g/3½oz ball)

- 1 ball of 07 turquoise (A)
- 1 ball of 03 cream (B)
- 1 ball of 101 dark orange (C)

Hooks and Notions
6mm (US J/10) crochet hook

Tapestry needle

Tape measure

Approx. 29cm x 17cm (11½in x 6¾in) and 29cm x 12cm (11½in x 4¾in) pieces of lining fabric

Pins

Sewing needle and matching thread

2m (2yds) length of 1.5cm (⅝in) wide cotton webbing

3 black sequins

Tension
12 sts and 13 rows to 10cm (4in) measured over double crochet

Finished Size
30cm (11¾in) x 18cm (7in)

Abbreviations
See page 125.

Pattern Notes
This pattern uses the Tapestry Crochet technique (see page 122), meaning you carry all the colours in use.

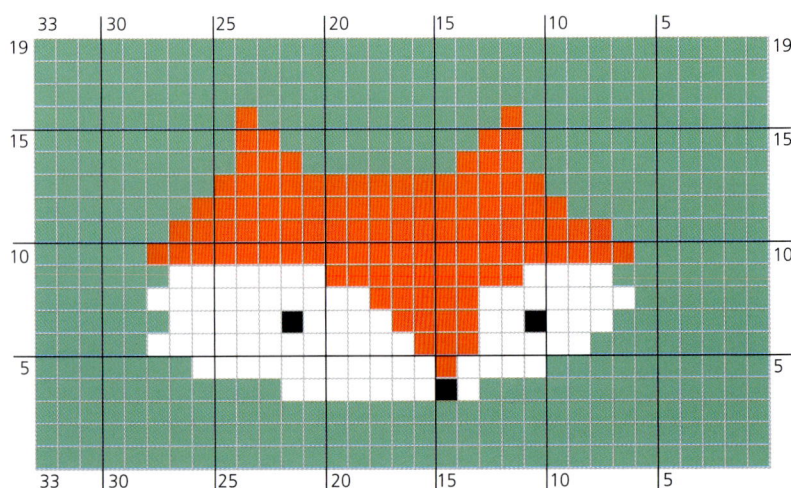

Key
- turquoise (A)
- cream (B)
- dark orange (C)
- sequin placement

For the Case

Using yarn A and 6mm (US J/10) hook, make 34ch.

Foundation row: 1dc in second ch from hook (missed ch does not count as st), 1dc in each ch to end, turn. *(33 sts)*

Commence Tapestry Crochet pattern (see page 122). Work in dc changing colour as indicated and carrying the unused yarn across the back. The number indicates the amount of stitches and the letter denotes the yarn colour. For example; 5A, 4B, 5A means work 5dc in A, 4dc in B, 5dc in A.

Note: Work the sequin placement squares in yarn B and stitch sequins in place once complete.

Rows 1–3: 33A.
Row 4: 13A, 9B, 11A.
Row 5: 7A, 11B, 1C, 4B, 10A.
Row 6: 8A, 5B, 3C, 12B, 5A.
Row 7: 6A, 10B, 4C, 6B, 7A.
Row 8: 6A, 7B, 5C, 10B, 5A.
Row 9: 6A, 7B, 9C, 4B, 7A.

Row 10: 6A, 22C, 5A.
Row 11: 6A, 20C, 7A.
Row 12: 9A, 17C, 7A.
Row 13: 8A, 15C, 10A.
Row 14: 11A, 3C, 7A, 3C, 9A.
Row 15: 9A, 2C, 9A, 2C, 11A.
Row 16: 11A, 1C, 11A, 1C, 9A.
Row 17: 33A.

Leaving Yarn B attached, fasten off all other yarns.

Edging: Using Yarn B, work 1ch, then 1dc in each st and row-end around entire piece, working 3dc in each corner. Fasten off.

Making Up and Finishing

Weave in all loose ends and block to measurements.

Stitch sequins in place for the eyes and nose (see Chart).

For the Lining

Hem one long edge of the smaller piece of fabric. Lay it over the bottom half of the larger piece of fabric, with the hemmed edge in the middle, and pin into place. Mark 8 spaces 3cm (1¹⁄₁₆in) wide across and stitch in vertical lines from the hemmed edge to the bottom edge to make each narrow pocket, leaving a larger pocket at one end for tape measures and such like.

Hem the whole piece so it measures approx. 28cm x 16cm (11in x 6¼in).

Fold the webbing in half and tack the folded end to the back of the crocheted piece. Place the finished lining on top and hand sew into place.

This very tactile and extremely pretty purse has the remarkable effect of demanding to be used. It's such a treat to pop your hand in your bag to look for something and feel the silky yarn under your fingers, and the variegated colours also make the simple, repetitive pattern shine beautifully.

little purse

Yarn
Debbie Bliss Luxury Silk DK (DK weight; 100% silk; 100m/109yds per 50g/1¾oz ball)
  1 ball of shade 048 Lavender

Hooks and Notions
4mm (US G/6) crochet hook
Tapestry needle
9cm (3½in) wide horseshoe purse clasp

Tension
19 sts and 25 rows to 10cm (4in) measured over double crochet

Finished Size
9cm (3½in) wide x 11cm (4¼in) deep

Abbreviations
See page 125.

TIP Different clasps can change the whole look of your finished make. It's worth going shopping with your intended yarn and picking one that really sets off the colours.

For the Bag
Using yarn A and 4mm (US G/6) hook, make 17ch.
Round 1: 2dc in second ch from hook (missed ch does not count as st), 1dc in each of next 14 ch, 3dc in end ch. Working along the opposite side of the ch, work 1dc in each of next 14 ch, 1dc in last ch (same st as initial 2dc), sl st in first dc to join. *(34 sts)*
Round 2: 1ch (does not count as st throughout), 2dc in first st, 1dc in next 16 sts, 2dc in next st, 1dc in next 16 sts, join with a sl st in first dc. *(36 sts)*
Round 3: 1ch, 2dc in next st, 1dc in next 17 sts, 2dc in next st, 1dc in next 17 sts, join with a sl st in first dc. *(38 sts)*
Round 4: 1ch, 2dc in first st, 1dc in next 18 sts, 2dc in next st, 1dc in next 18 sts, join with a sl st in first dc. *(40 sts)*
Round 5 (star stitch): 3ch, pull up a loop in second ch from hook, pull up a loop in third ch from hook, pull up a loop in each of next 2 sts, yrh and pull through all 5 loops on hook, 1ch to close the star, *pull up a loop in centre of star last star made, pull up a loop around bottom left post/stitch of the star, pull up a loop in each of next 2 sts, yrh and pull through all 5 loops on hook, 1ch to close; rep from * to end, join with sl st in centre of first star.
Round 6: 2ch (does not count as st throughout), work 2htr in centre of each star around, join with sl st in first htr.
Rounds 7–12: Rep Rounds 6–7, ending with Round 6.
Now work in rows to form one side of the top section:
Row 1: 2ch, 1htr in next 16 sts, turn. *(16 sts)*
Row 2: 2ch, htr2tog, 1htr in next 12 sts, htr2tog, turn. *(14 sts)*
Row 3: 2ch, htr2tog, 1htr in next 10 sts, htr2tog, turn. *(12 sts)*
Row 4: 2ch, htr2tog, 1htr in next 8 sts, htr2tog, turn. *(10 sts)*
Row 5: 2ch, htr2tog, 1htr in next 6 sts, htr2tog, turn. *(8 sts)*
Fasten off.
Count 4 sts along from end of Row 1. Rejoin yarn and rep Rows 1–5 for opposite side. Fasten off.

Making Up and Finishing
Weave in loose ends and very gently steam block the purse.

Using the working yarn, whip stitch (see page 118) the clasp in place.

I have to thank the very talented and generous Loes (aka @Pomenco on Instagram) for the loan of this excellent hexagon pattern. Based on a traditional quilting motif, this little hexagon has the same stunning effect with none of the sewing.

geometric pencil case

Skill Level ✶ ✶ ✶

Yarn

DMC Natura Just Cotton (4-ply weight; 100% cotton; 155m/169yds per 50g/1¾oz ball)

- 1 ball of 62 Cerise (A)
- 1 ball of 47 Safran (B)
- 1 ball of 43 Golden Lemon (C)

Hooks and Notions

3.25mm (US D/3) crochet hook

Tapestry needle

Sewing needle and matching thread

Approx. 23.5cm x 26.56cm (9¼in x 10½in) piece of fabric

20cm (8in) zip

Tension

1 hexagon to measure 4.5cm (1¾in)

Finished Size

22cm (8¾in) wide x 12.5cm (5in) deep

Abbreviations

See page 125.

Pattern Notes

This pattern is constructed from 17 hexagons sewn together and then mounted onto a fabric case.

For the Hexagons (make 17 alike)

Using yarn A and 3.25mm (US D/3) hook, make 5ch, sl st in first ch to form a ring.

Round 1: 3ch (counts as 1tr throughout), working into the ring, 1tr, 2ch, 2tr, 1ch, change to yarn B, 1ch, 2tr, 2ch, 2tr, 1ch, change to yarn C, 1ch, 2tr, 2ch, 2tr, 1ch, change to yarn A, 1ch, 1, sl st in third ch of 3ch to join.

Round 2: Using yarn A, 3ch, 1tr in next st, [2tr, 2ch, 2tr] in ch-sp, 1tr in next 2 sts, 1tr in ch-sp, 1ch, *change to yarn B, 1ch, 1tr in ch-sp, 1tr in next 2 sts, [2tr, 2ch, 2tr] in ch-sp, 1tr in next 2 sts, 1tr in ch-sp, 1ch; rep from * once more using yarn C, change to yarn A, 1ch, 1tr in ch-sp, sl st in third ch of 3ch to join.

Fasten off.

Making Up and Finishing

Weave in all loose ends and block to measurements.

Lay the hexagons out as follows:

Row 1: 6 hexagons.

Row 2: 5 hexagons.

Row 3: 6 hexagons.

Sew together working through the back loops of the stitches – from the front you won't see anything.

Fold under the sides of the hexagons at the ends of the top and bottom rows and stitch down.

For the Fabric Case

Fold the fabric in half widthways and sew up the side edges. Hem the top edge and insert zip. Hand sew the hexagon piece to the front of the case.

I love the wonders of modern technology, but can be quite clumsy with my precious gadgets, so I decided it was time to make a case to protect my reading tablet. The eye-catching design means I don't forget to use it!

tablet case

Skill Level ★ ★ ☆

Yarn

Cascade 220 (Aran; 100% Peruvian Highland wool; 200m/220yds per 100g/3½oz skein)

1 skein of 9478 Cotton Candy (A)
1 skein of 7814 Chartreuse (B)
1 skein of 8687 Butter (C)
1 skein of 9615 Bright Nectarine (D)
1 skein of 8906 Blue Topaz (E)

Hooks and Notions

5mm (US H/8) crochet hook

Tension

20 sts and 17 rows to 10cm (4in) measured over tapestry double crochet

Finished Size

12cm (4¾in) x 18cm (7in)

You can adjust the size to fit your tablet by making making more chain stitches at the start or by continuing to crochet more rounds.

Abbreviations

See page 125.

Pattern Notes

When worked in the round a tapestry design will naturally slant.

TIP The case is worked in a spiral; use a locking stitch marker to keep track of the first stitch, moving it up as each round is completed.

For the Case

Using yarn E and 5mm (US H/8) hook, make 49ch.

Set-up round: 1dc in second ch from hook (missed ch does not count as st), 1dc in each ch to end, join with a sl st in first dc. *(48 sts)*

Commence Tapestry Crochet pattern (see page 122) and work in dc changing colour as indicated and working stitches over the unused yarn as you go. The number indicates the amount of stitches and the letter denotes the yarn colour. For example; 5A, 4B, 5A means work 5dc in A, 4dc in B, 5dc in A.

Round 1: *1A, 3B; rep from * around.
Round 2: *2A, 2B; rep from * around.
Round 3: *3A, 1B; rep from * around.
Round 4: *3C, 1D; rep from * around.
Round 5: *2C, 2D; rep from * around.
Round 6: *1C, 3D; rep from * around.
Rounds 7–9: Using yarns B and E, rep Rounds 1–3.
Rounds 10–12: Using yarns A and C, rep Rows 4–6.
Rounds 13–15: Using yarns E and D, rep Rows 1–3.
Rounds 16–18: Using yarns B and A, rep Rows 4–6.
Rounds 19–21: Using yarns D and C, rep Rows 1–3.
Rounds 22–24: Using yarns E and B, rep Rows 4–6.
Rounds 25–27: Using yarns C and A, rep Rows 1–3.
Round 28: Using yarn E only, work 1dc in each st, join with a sl st in last first dc.
Fasten off.

Making Up and Finishing

Weave in loose ends and block to measurements.

Whip stitch (see page 118) one end closed.

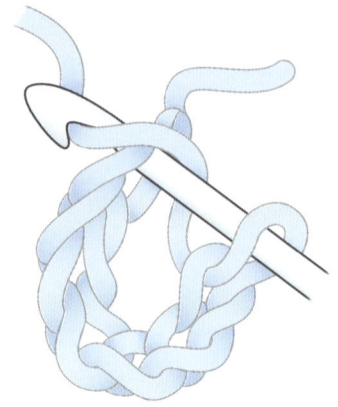

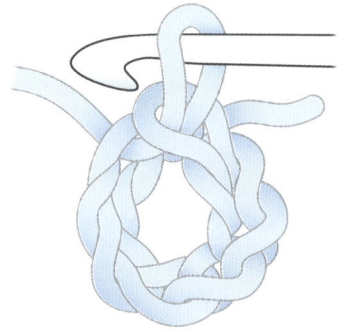

techniques

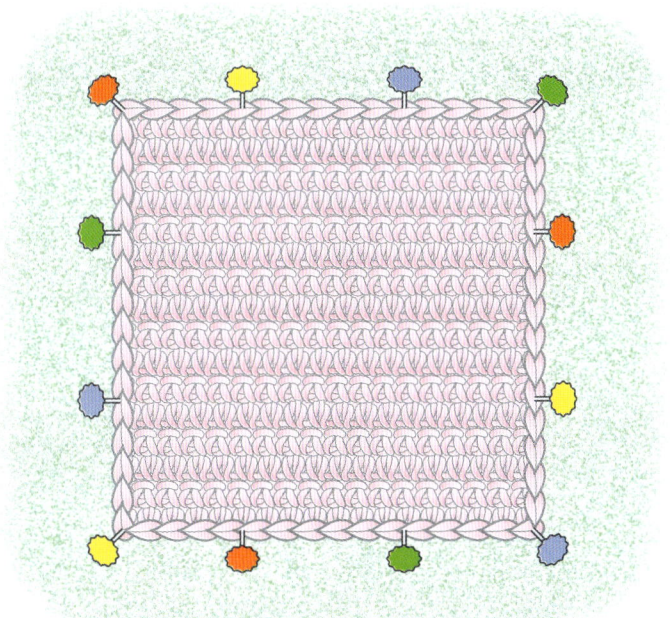

Holding the hook

Pick up your hook as though you are picking up a pen or pencil. Keeping the hook held loosely between your fingers and thumb, turn your hand so that the palm is facing up and the hook is balanced in your hand and resting in the space between your index finger and your thumb.

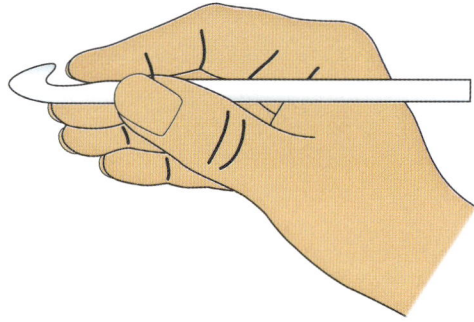

Holding the yarn

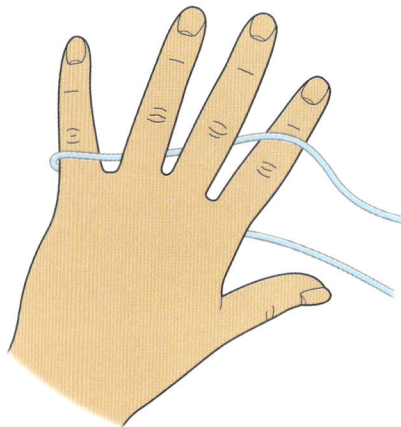

1 Pick up the yarn with your little finger in the opposite hand to your hook, with your palm facing upwards and with the short end in front. Turn your hand to face downwards, with the yarn on top of your index finger and under the other two fingers and wrapped right around the little finger, as shown above.

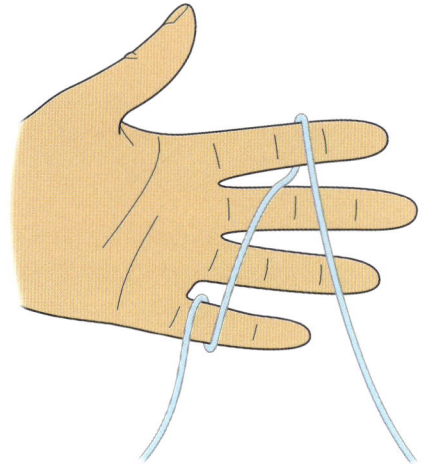

2 Turn your hand to face you, ready to hold the work in your middle finger and thumb. Keeping your index finger only at a slight curve, hold the work or the slip knot using the same hand, between your middle finger and your thumb and just below the crochet hook and loop/s on the hook.

Holding your hook and yarn while crocheting

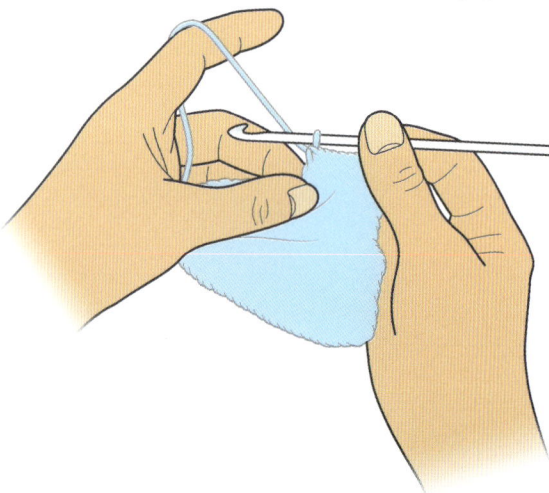

Keep your index finger, with the yarn draped over it, at a slight curve, and hold your work (or the slip knot) using the same hand, between your middle finger and your thumb and just below the crochet hook and the loop/s on the hook.

As you draw the loop through the hook, release the yarn on the index finger to allow the loop to stay loose on the hook. If you tense your index finger, the yarn will become too tight and pull the loop on the hook too tight for you to draw the yarn through.

Some left-handers learn to crochet like right-handers, but others learn with everything reversed – with the hook in the left hand and the yarn in the right.

Yarn round hook (yrh)

To create a stitch, catch the yarn from behind with the hook pointing upwards. As you gently pull the yarn through the loop on the hook, turn the hook so it faces downwards and slide the yarn through the loop. The loop on the hook should be kept loose enough for the hook to slide through easily.

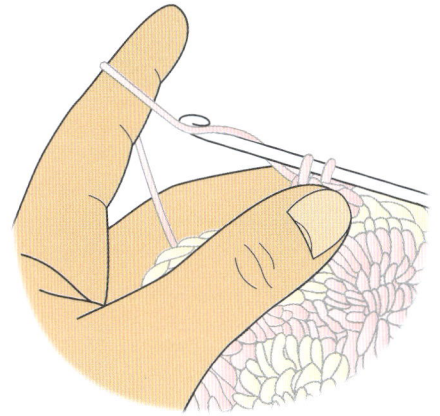

Making a slip knot

The simplest way is to make a circle with the yarn, so that the loop is facing downwards.

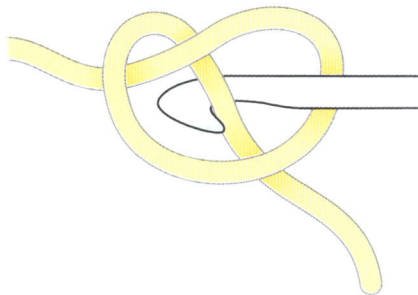

1 In one hand hold the circle at the top where the yarn crosses, and let the tail drop down at the back so that it falls across the center of the loop. With your free hand or the tip of a crochet hook, pull a loop through the circle.

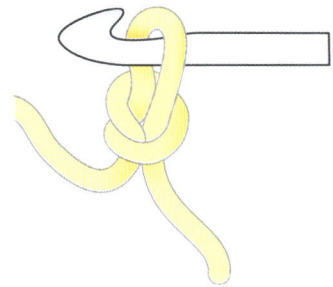

2 Put the hook into the loop and pull gently so that it forms a loose loop on the hook.

Magic ring

This is a useful starting technique if you do not want a visible hole in the centre of your round. Loop the yarn around your finger, insert the hook through the ring, yarn round hook, and pull through the ring to make the first chain. Work the number of stitches required into the ring and then pull the end to tighten the centre ring and close the hole.

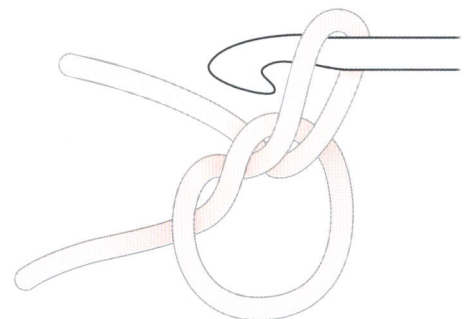

Chain (ch)

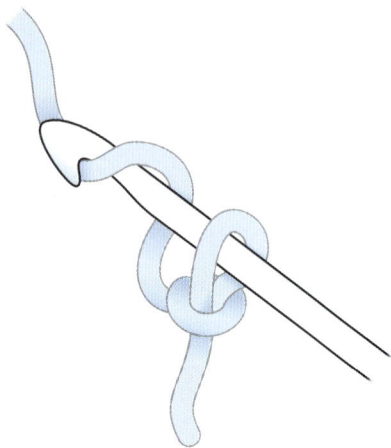

1 Using the hook, wrap the yarn round the hook ready to pull it through the loop on the hook.

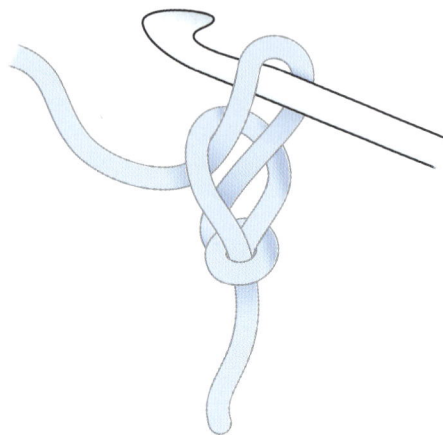

2 Pull through, creating a new loop on the hook. Continue in this way to create a chain of the required length.

Chain ring

If you are crocheting a round shape, one way of starting off is by crocheting a number of chains following the instructions in your pattern, and then joining them into a circle.

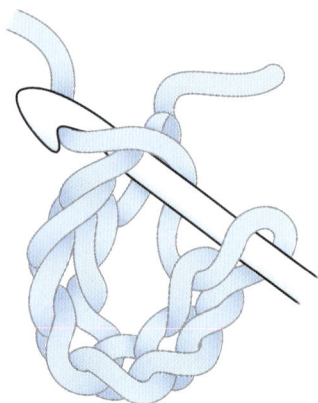

1 To join the chain into a circle, insert the crochet hook into the first chain that you made (not into the slip knot), yarn round hook.

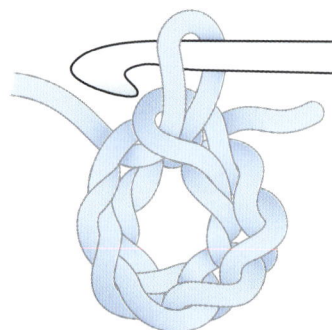

2 Pull the yarn through the chain and through the loop on your hook at the same time, thereby creating a slip stitch and forming a circle. You now have a chain ring ready to work stitches into as instructed in the pattern.

Chain space (ch-sp)

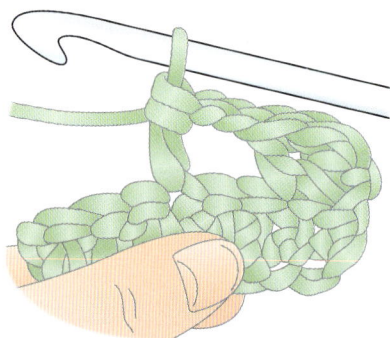

1 A chain space is the space that has been made under a chain in the previous round or row, and falls in between other stitches.

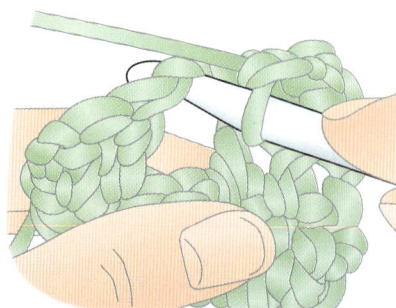

2 Stitches into a chain space are made directly into the hole created under the chain and not into the chain stitches themselves.

Working into both sides of the foundation chain

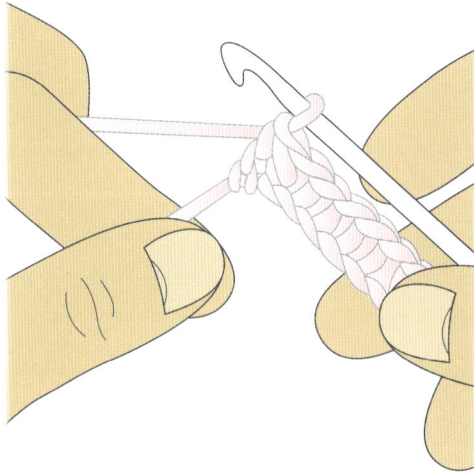

1 Make the required number of starting chains and work stitches as instructed in the pattern – you will be working a stitch into each chain and multiple stitches into the end chain.

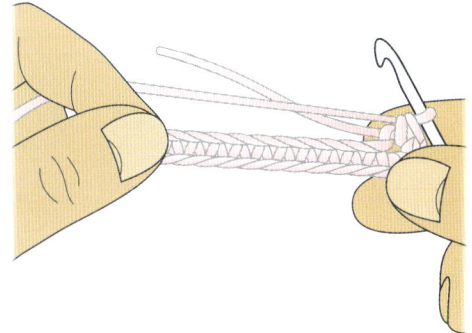

2 Turn the chain 180 degrees clockwise.

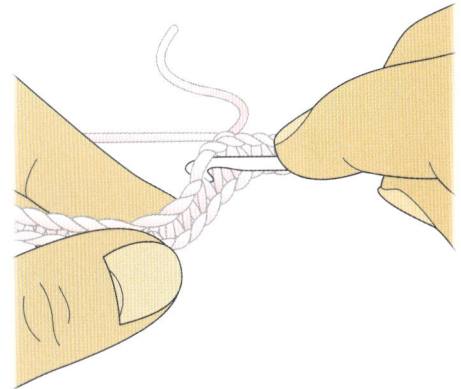

3 Work a stitch into each chain again along the other side of the foundation chain, and multiple stitches into the end chain. Slip stitch to join for working in the round.

Slip stitch (sl st)

A slip stitch doesn't create any height and is often used as the last stitch to create a smooth and even round or row.

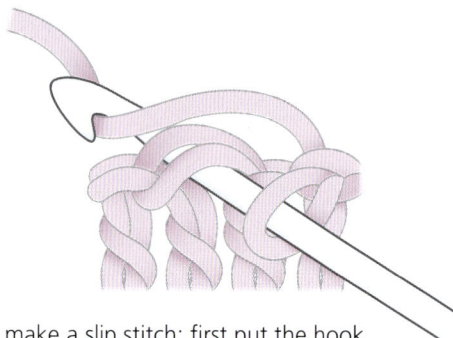

1 To make a slip stitch: first put the hook through the work, yarn round hook.

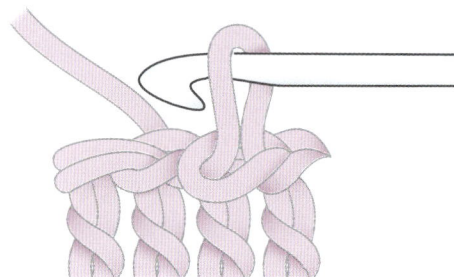

2 Pull the yarn through both the work and through the loop on the hook at the same time, so you will have 1 loop on the hook.

Making rounds

When working in rounds the work is not turned, so you are always working from one side. Depending on the pattern you are working, a 'round' can be square.

Start each round by making one or more chains to create the height you need for the stitch you are working:

Double crochet = 1 chain

Half treble crochet = 2 chains

Treble crochet = 3 chains

Work the required stitches to complete the round. At the end of the round, slip stitch into the top of the chain to close the round.

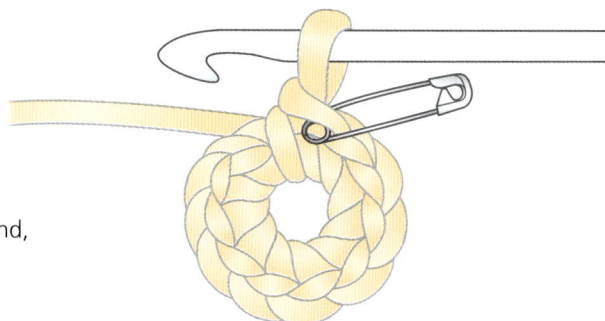

If you work in a spiral you do not need a turning chain. After completing the base ring, place a stitch marker in the first stitch and then continue to crochet around. When you have made a round and reached the point where the stitch marker is, work this stitch, take out the stitch marker from the previous round and put it back into the first stitch of the new round. A safety pin, or piece of yarn in a contrasting colour, makes a good stitch marker.

Making rows

When making straight rows you turn the work at the end of each row and make a turning chain to create the height you need for the stitch you are working with, as for making rounds.

Double crochet = 1 chain

Half treble crochet = 2 chains

Treble crochet = 3 chains

Joining in the middle of a row

Sometimes you will need to join in a new yarn in the middle of the row, either because the yarn has run out and you need to use the same colour but with a new ball, or when instructed in the pattern to change colour. In this case you work part of the stitch in the old yarn and then switch to the new yarn to complete it, as explained in the instructions for joining a new yarn in double crochet.

Joining new yarn at the end of a row or round

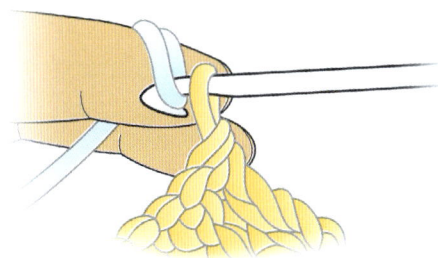

1 Keep the loop of the old yarn on the hook. Drop the tail and catch a loop of the strand of the new yarn with the crochet hook.

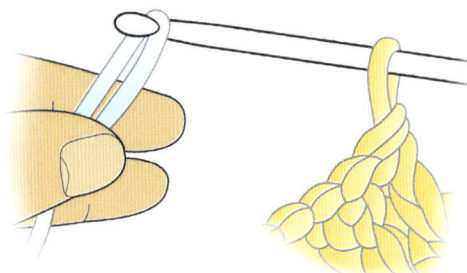

2 Pull the new yarn through the loop on the hook, keeping the old loop drawn tight.

Joining new yarn in double crochet

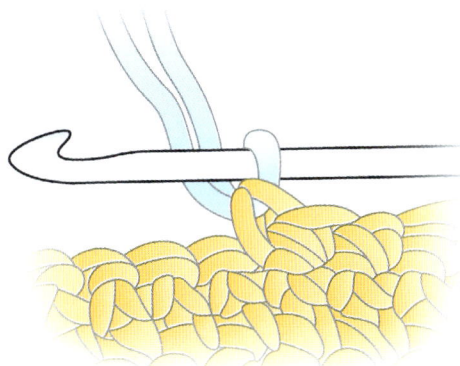

1 Make a double crochet stitch as usual, but do not complete the stitch. When there are two loops remaining on the hook, drop the old yarn, catch the new yarn with the hook and pull it through these two loops to complete the stitch.

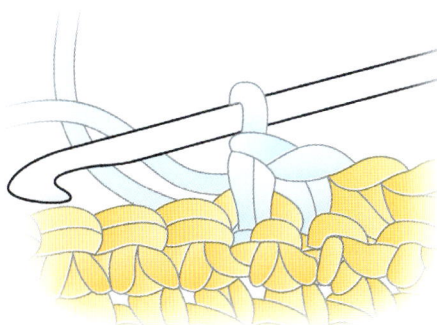

2 Continue to crochet with the new yarn. Cut the strand of the old yarn about 15cm (6in) from the crochet and leave it to drop at the back of the work so you can sew this end in later.

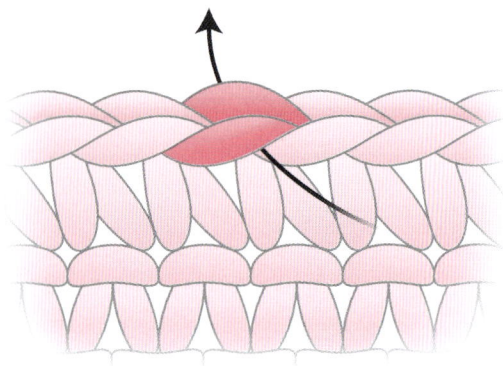

Working into top of stitch

Unless otherwise directed, insert the hook under both of the two loops on top of the stitch – this is the standard technique.

Working into front loop of stitch (FLO)

To work into the front loop of a stitch, pick up the front loop from underneath at the front of the work.

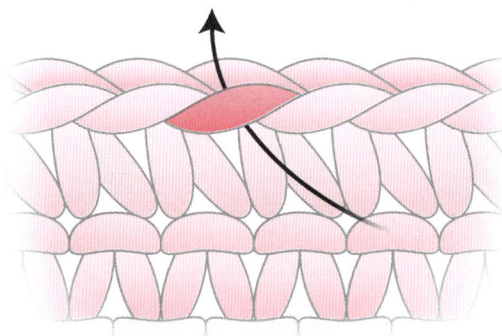

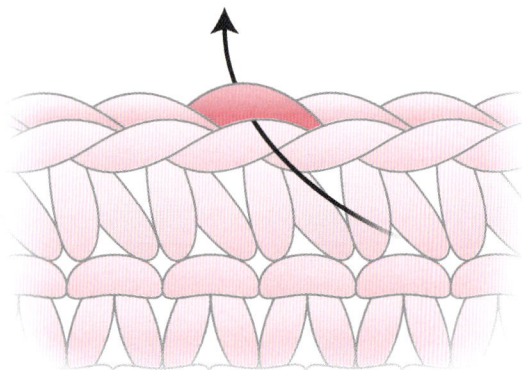

Working into back loop of stitch (BLO)

To work into the back loop of the stitch, insert the hook between the front and the back loop, picking up the back loop from the front of the work.

How to measure a tension square

Using the hook and the yarn recommended in the pattern, make a number of chains to measure approximately 15cm (6in). Working in the stitch pattern given for the tension measurements, work enough rows to form a square. Fasten off.

Take a ruler, place it horizontally across the square, and using pins, mark a 10cm (4in) area. Repeat vertically to form a 10cm (4in) square on the fabric.

Count the number of stitches across, and the number of rows within the square, and compare against the tension given in the pattern.

If your numbers match the pattern then use this size hook and yarn for your project. If you have more stitches, then your tension is tighter than recommended and you need to use a larger hook. If you have fewer stitches, then your tension is looser and you will need a smaller hook.

Make tension squares using different size hooks until you have matched the tension in the pattern, and use this hook to make the project.

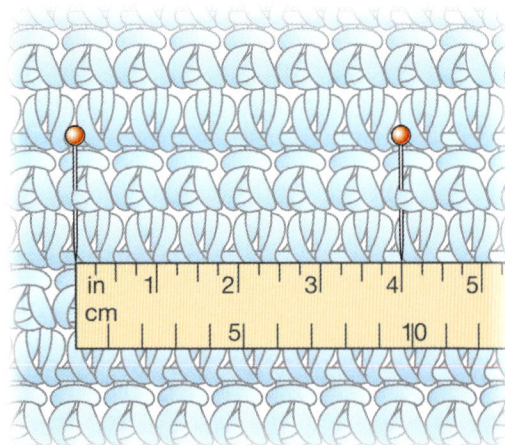

Double crochet (dc)

1 Insert the hook into your work, yarn round hook and pull the yarn through the work only. You will then have 2 loops on the hook.

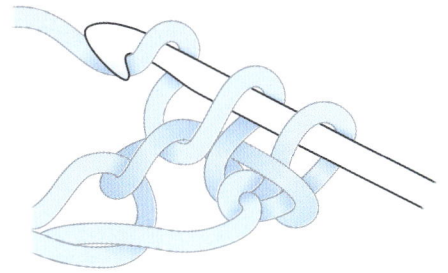

2 Yarn round hook again and pull through the two loops on the hook. You will then have 1 loop on the hook.

Half treble crochet (htr)

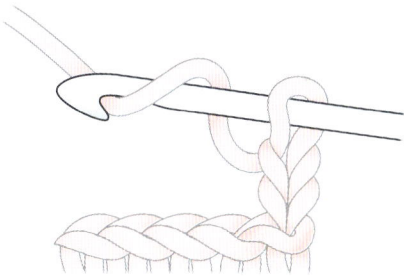

1 Before inserting the hook into the work, wrap the yarn round the hook and put the hook through the work with the yarn wrapped around.

2 Yarn round hook again and pull through the first loop on the hook. You now have 3 loops on the hook.

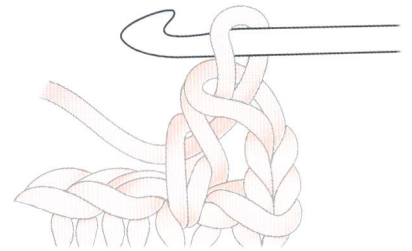

3 Yarn round hook and pull the yarn through all 3 loops. You will be left with 1 loop on the hook.

Double crochet (right side)

Half treble crochet (right side)

Treble (tr)

1 Before inserting the hook into the work, wrap the yarn round the hook. Put the hook through the work with the yarn wrapped around, yarn round hook again and pull through the first loop on the hook. You now have 3 loops on the hook.

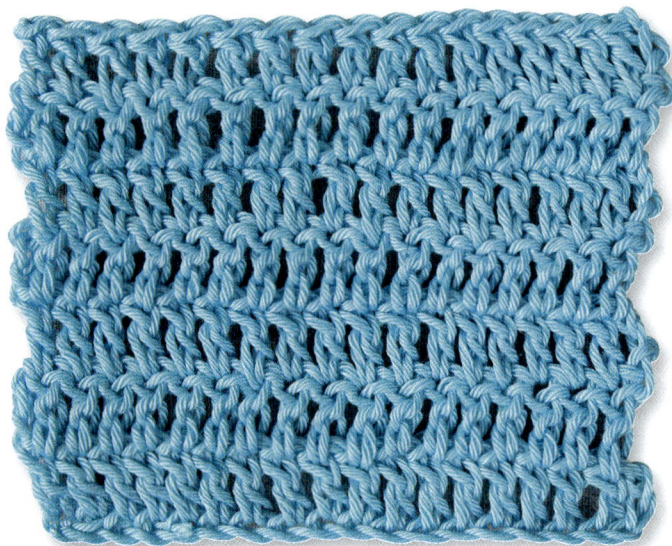

Treble crochet (right side)

2 Yarn round hook again, pull the yarn through the first 2 loops on the hook. You now have 2 loops on the hook.

3 Pull the yarn through 2 loops again. You will be left with 1 loop on the hook. The height of each stitch is called a 'post'.

Double treble (dtr)

Yarn round hook twice, insert hook into the stitch, yarn round hook, pull a loop through (4 loops on hook), yarn round hook, pull the yarn through 2 stitches (3 loops on hook), yarn round hook, pull a loop through the next 2 stitches (2 loops on hook), yarn round hook, pull a loop through the last 2 stitches.

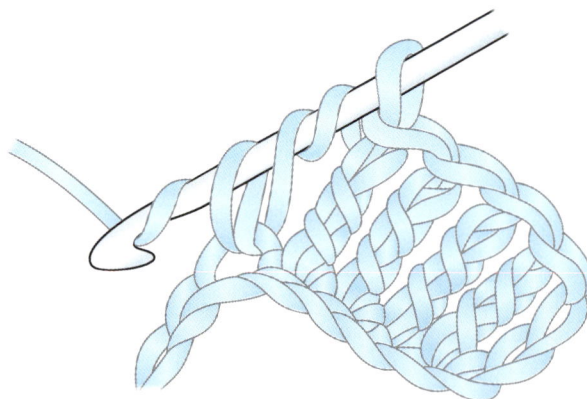

Increasing

Make two or three stitches into one stitch or space from the previous row. The illustration shows a treble crochet increase being made.

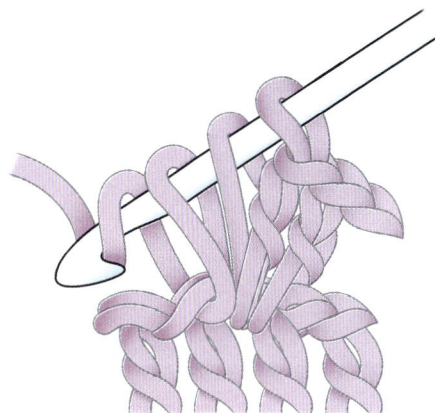

Decreasing

You can decrease by either missing the next stitch and continuing to crochet, or by crocheting two or more stitches together. The basic technique for crocheting stitches together is the same, no matter which stitch you are using. The following example shows dc2tog.

Double crochet two stitches together

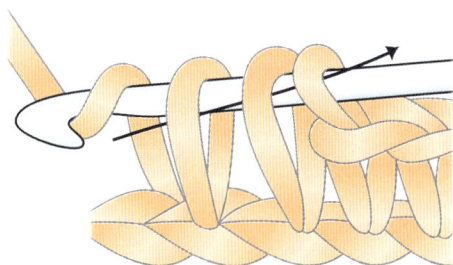

(dc2tog)

1 Insert the hook into your work, yarn round hook and pull the yarn through the work (2 loops on hook). Insert the hook in next stitch, yarn round hook and pull the yarn through (3 loops on hook).

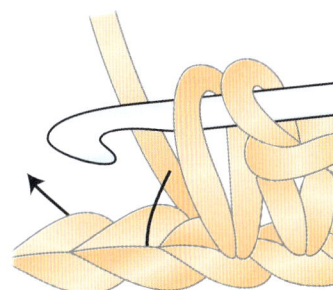

2 Yarn round hook again and pull through all 3 loops on the hook. You will then have 1 loop on the hook.

Changing colours

Note: You can use this technique when joining in a new ball of yarn as one runs out.

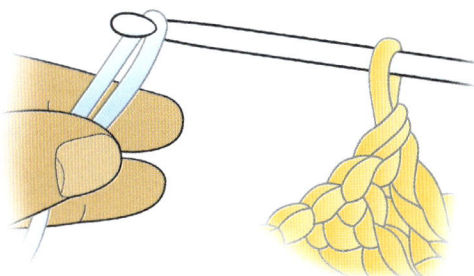

1 Keep the loop of the old yarn on the hook. Drop the tail and catch a loop of the strand of the new yarn with the crochet hook.

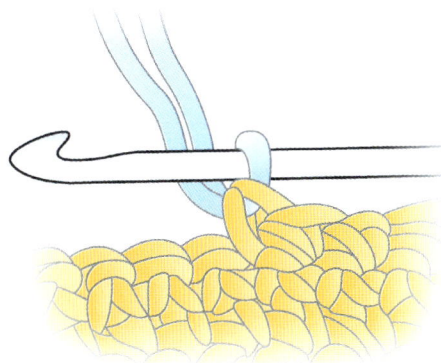

2 Pull the new yarn through the loop on the hook, keeping the old loop drawn tight and continue as instructed in the pattern.

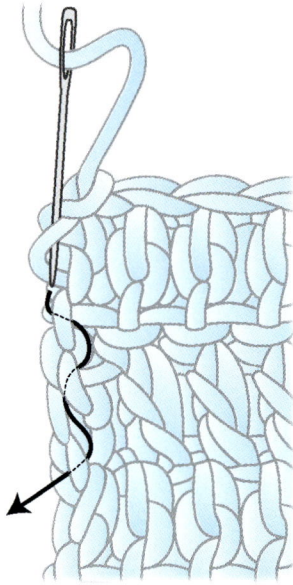

Weaving in yarn ends

It is important to weave in the tail ends of the yarn so that they are secure and your crochet won't unravel. Thread a tapestry needle with the tail end of yarn. On the wrong side, take the needle through the crochet one stitch down on the edge, then take it through the stitches, working in a gentle zigzag. Work through four or five stitches then return in the opposite direction. Remove the needle, pull the crochet gently to stretch it, and trim the end.

Blocking

Crochet can tend to curl so to make flat pieces stay flat you may need to block them. Pin the piece out to the correct size and shape on the ironing board, then cover with a cloth and press or steam gently (depending on the type of yarn) and allow to dry completely.

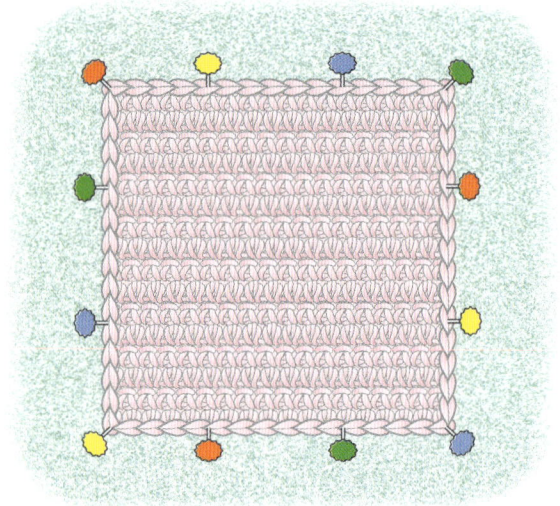

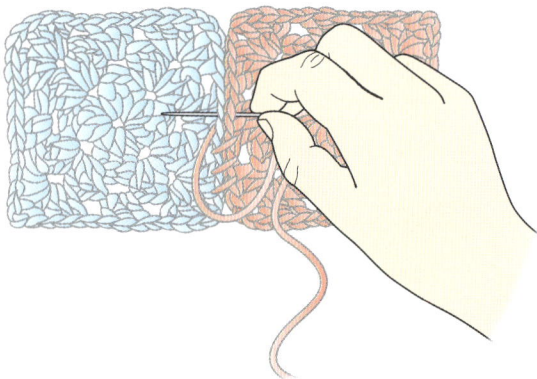

Sewing up

Whip Stitch: Sewing up crochet fabric can be done in many ways, but using a whip stitch is the easiest. However, you will be able to see the stitches clearly, so use a matching yarn. Lay the two pieces to be joined next to each other with right sides facing upwards. Secure the yarn to one piece. Insert the needle into the front of one piece of fabric, then up from the back of the adjoining fabric. Repeat along the seam.

Mattress Stitch is made by picking up the loops or bars, either one stitch in or at the inside edge of the edging stitch of the first crochet piece, and then picking up the bars from the corresponding stitch on the second piece. If you're sewing together a piece without uniform stitches it's not always obvious where to put the needle. If you're sewing up a piece crocheted in single crochet or double crochet – something that is uniform in shape – it's easier to see where the bars are.

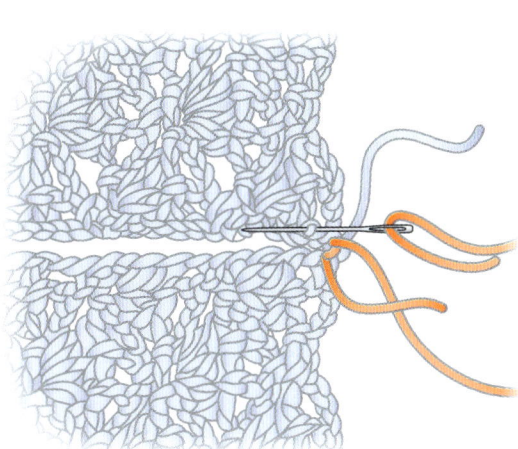

1 Line up the two pieces to be joined, with right sides facing you. Thread a tail of yarn, in the same colour as the pieces you're joining, into a yarn sewing needle. Pick up a loop on the other side with the yarn sewing needle at a horizontal (90 degree) angle to the pattern and draw the yarn through loosely.

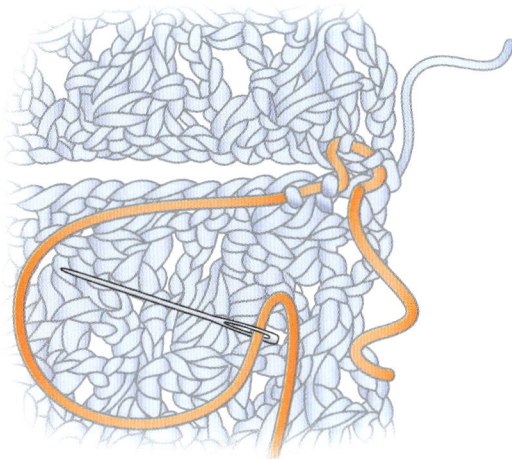

2 Pick up a loop on the corresponding side of the other piece just inside the edge and draw through the yarn. Leave the loops loose and don't draw them through tightly. Pick up the next loop approx. 1 cm (½ in) along on the same side and draw through the yarn.

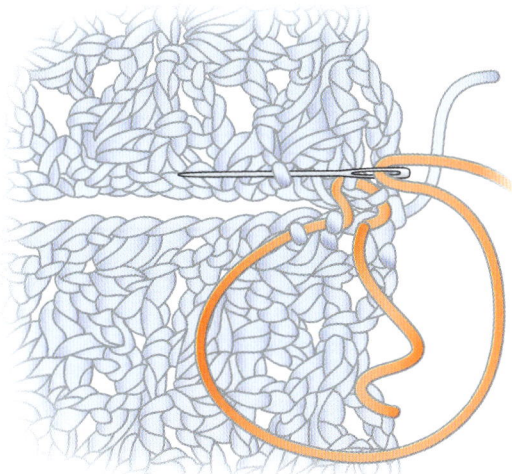

3 Pick up a loop on the corresponding side of the other piece just inside the edge and draw through the yarn. Leave the loops loose and don't draw them through tightly.

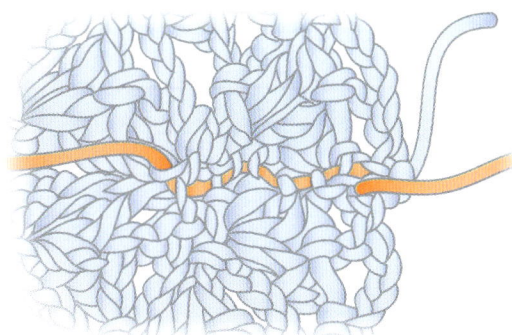

4 Repeat steps 2 and 3. When you have about 6 loops, hold the pieces firmly in place and pull the thread to draw the loose loops and bind the edging together. Continue in this way until the pieces are joined. This will create an invisible seam on the right side of the work.

Sewing on buttons

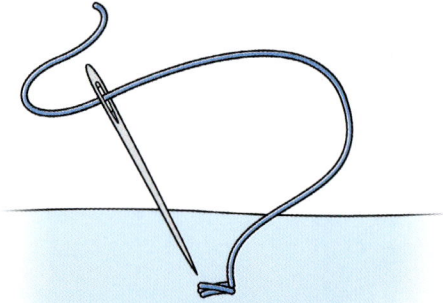

1 Mark the place where you want the button to go. Push the needle up from the back of the fabric and sew a few stitches over and over in this place.

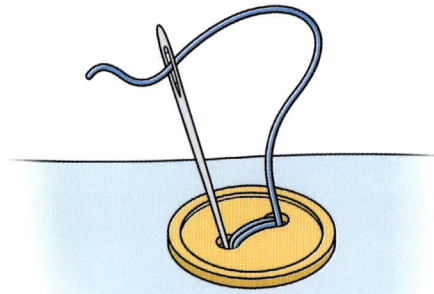

2 Now bring the needle up through one of the holes in the button. Push the needle back down through the second hole and through the fabric. Bring it back up through the first hole. Repeat this five or six times. If there are four holes in the button, use all four of them to make a cross pattern. Make sure that you keep the stitches close together under the middle of the button.

3 Finish with a few small stitches over and over on the back of the fabric and trim the thread.

Tassels and fringes

1 Cut yarn to quantity and length given in the pattern. Take suggested bundle of strands and fold in half. With right side of project facing, insert a crochet hook from the wrong side through one of the edge stitches. Catch the bunch of strands with the hook at the fold point.

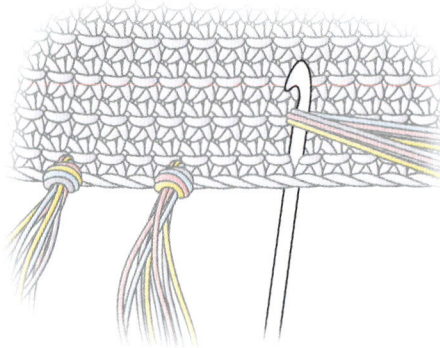

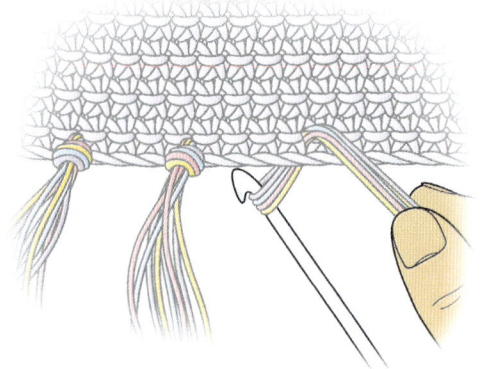

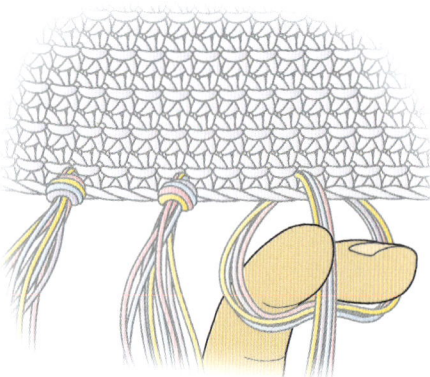

2 Pull through to make a big loop and, using your fingers, pull the tails of the bunch of strands through the loop.

3 Pull on the tails to tighten the loop firmly to secure the tassel.

Lining a bag with fabric

It's not always necessary to line a crochet bag, especially when tapestry crochet is used, but in some projects you will need to make a lining. Specific instructions are given in the projects, but the general method is given here.

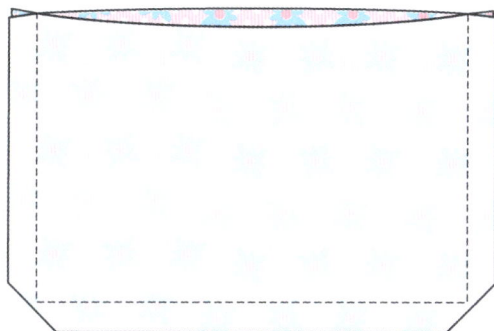

1 Cut two pieces of lining fabric to the same size as the bag plus an extra 1.5cm (⅝in) allowance for seams on the sides and bottom and an extra 2.5cm (1in) at the top. Pin the fabric pieces right sides together and machine sew the side and bottom seams. Trim across the bottom corners and press out the seams.

2 Turn the top edge of the lining over to the wrong side by 2.5cm (1in) and press.

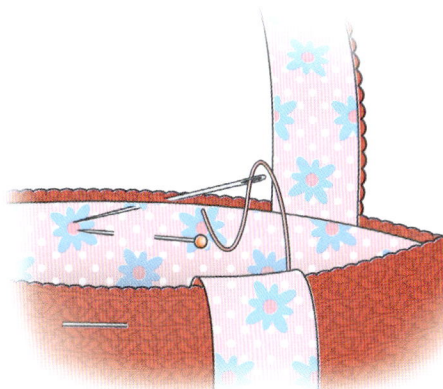

3 Insert the lining into the bag with wrong sides of crochet and lining together and pin in place around the top edge. Hand-sew the lining to the crocheted piece around the top edge, stitching across the handles if they are being inserted between the lining and the bag.

How to Tapestry Crochet

Tapestry crochet involves carrying one or more additional colours through the work until you are ready to use them. This is the crochet equivalent of Fair Isle or stranding, but with the bonus that the second colour is not visible at the back of the work – it is fully enclosed in the stitches of the first colour.

Carrying the second yarn

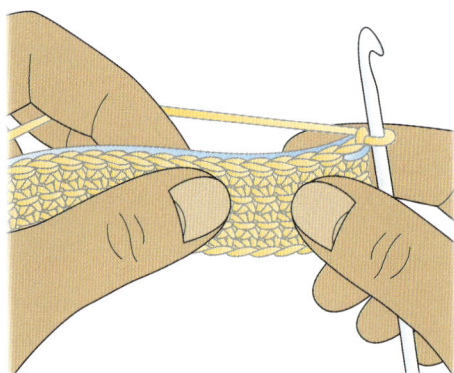

1 Hold the second colour yarn along the top of the stitches from the previous row. You can do this from the beginning of a row, or just join it in a few stitches before you need to start using the second colour, if it is only going to be used for a small area.

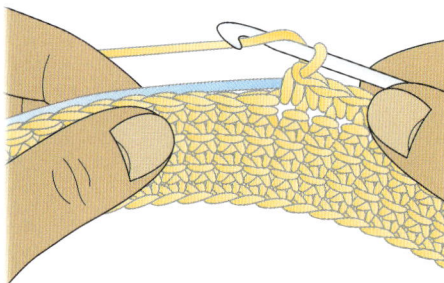

2 Work stitches in the normal way in the first colour, but going over the second colour and ensuring it is 'trapped' within the stitches. Continue working in this way, carrying the second colour until you are ready to work a stitch in it.

Changing colour in single crochet

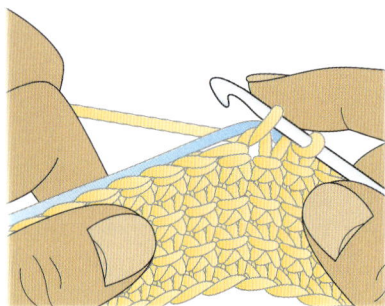

1 With the first colour, put the yarn through the next stitch, yarn over and pull through.

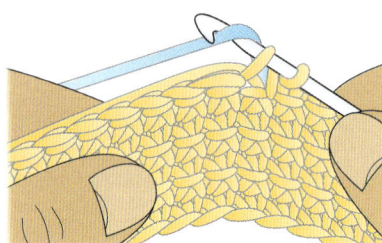

2 Using the second colour, yarn over hook.

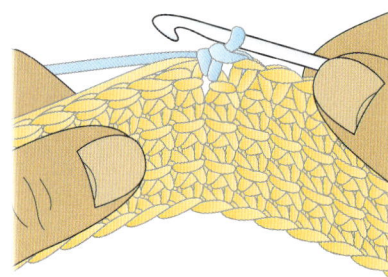

3 Pull the new colour yarn through both loops on the hook, to complete the stitch and change to the new colour. Continue in second colour, working over the first colour.

Turning at the end of a row

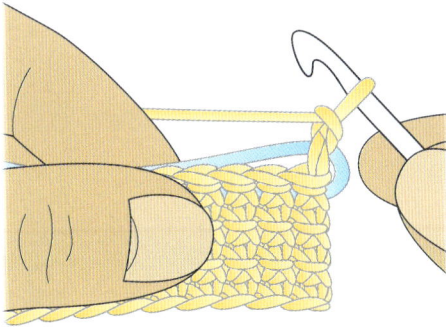

1 With the working colour, make the appropriate length turning chain. Pull the second yarn up, holding it tight along the top of your work.

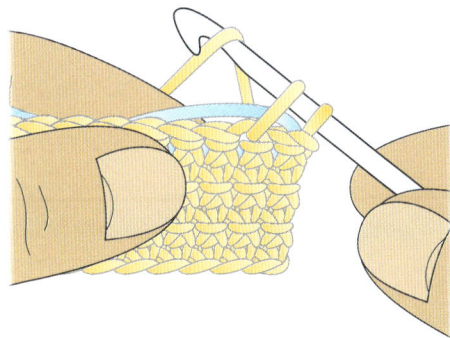

2 Work the next stitch over the second yarn, catching it behind the piece.

3 Continue to work over the second colour, as above.

Embroidery stitches

Some projects require detailing to be embroidered on to the crochet. Here are a few basic stitches you can use.

Backstitch

Work from right to left. Bring the needle up from the back of the fabric, one stitch length to the left of the end of the stitching line. Insert it one stitch length to the right, at the very end of the stitching line, and bring it up again one stitch length in front of the point from which it first emerged. Pull the thread through. To begin the next stitch, insert the needle at the left-hand end of the previous stitch. Continue to the end.

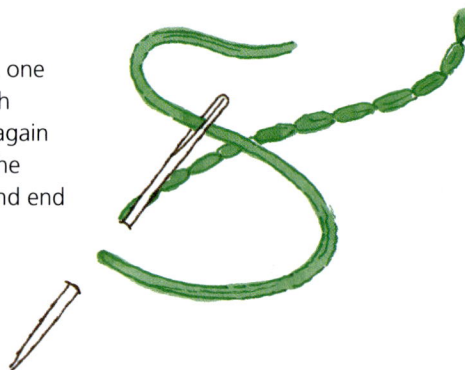

Chain stitch

Bring the needle out at the start of the stitching line. Re-insert it at the same point and bring it out a short distance away, looping the thread around the needle tip. Pull the thread through. For the next stitch, insert the needle right next to where it last emerged, just inside the loop of the previous chain, and bring it out a short distance away, again looping the thread around the needle tip. Fasten off at the end of the chain by taking a small vertical stitch across the bottom of the loop.

Cross stitch

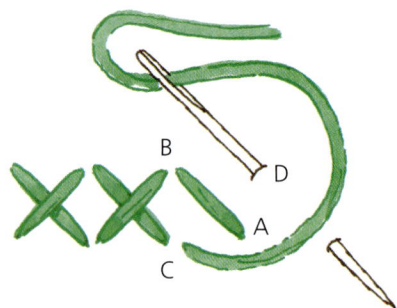

1 To work a single cross stitch, bring the needle up through the fabric at A and down at B, then up at C and down at D.

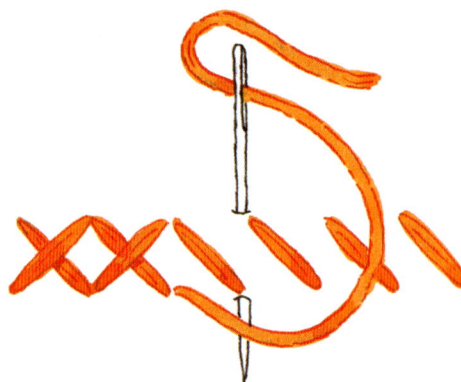

2 To work a row of cross stitches, work the diagonal stitches in one direction only, from right to left, then reverse the direction and work the second half of the stitch across each stitch made on the first journey.

Abbreviations

[ ]	Square parentheses indicate a repeat
*	Asterisk indicates where to repeat from
approx.	Approximately
BLO	Back loop only
cm	Centimeter(s)
ch	Chain
dc	Double crochet
dc2tog	Double crochet 2 stitches together
FLO	Front loop only
g	Gram(s)
htr	Half treble crochet
in	Inch(es)
m	Meter(s)
oz	Ounce(s)
rep	Repeat
RS	Right side of fabric
sk	Skip
sl st	Slip stitch
st(s)	Stitch(es)
tr	Treble
WS	Wrong side of fabric
yd(s)	Yard(s)
yrh	Yarn round hook

Crochet stitch conversion chart

Crochet stitches are worked in the same way in both the USA and the UK, but the stitch names are not the same and identical names are used for different stitches.

Below is a list of the UK terms used in this book, and the equivalent US terms.

UK TERM	US TERM
double crochet (dc)	single crochet (sc)
half treble (htr)	half double crochet (hdc)
treble (tr)	double crochet (dc)
double treble (dtr)	treble (tr)
triple treble (trtr)	double treble (dtr)
tension	gauge
yarn round hook (yrh)	yarn over hook (yoh)

suppliers

When making bags, the exact size of the finished product is not always crucial, so you can change yarns for something of a similar weight and yardage per ball. However, it is still worth doing a tension square where possible to make sure that the proportions will be roughly the same.

We cannot cover all stockists here, so please explore the local knitting stores and online retailers in your own country. If you wish to substitute a different yarn for the one recommended in the pattern, try the YarnSub website for suggestions: www.yarnsub.com

UK

Hobbycraft
Online sales and store locator
www.hobbycraft.co.uk
Sells Lion Brand, Rico, Sirdar

John Lewis
Online sales and store locator
www.johnlewis.com
Sells King Cole, Rico, Sirdar

LoveCrafts
Online sales only
www.lovecrafts.com
Sells Berroco, Cascade, Debbie Bliss, DMC, Hoooked, King Cole, Lion Brand, Nako, Rico, Sirdar

Wool Warehouse
Online sales and store
www.woolwarehouse.co.uk
Sells Caron, Cascade, DMC, King Cole, Lion Brand, Rico, Sirdar

USA AND CANADA

Diamond Yarn
Online sales and store
www.diamondyarn.ca
Sells Bergere de France, Debbie Bliss, Katia, Nako, Sirdar

JOANN
Online sales and store locator
www.joann.com
Sells Caron, DMC, Hoooked, Lion Brand

Knitting Fever Inc.
Online sales and stockist locator
www.knittingfever.com
Sells Katia

LoveCrafts
Online sales only
www.lovecrafts.com
Sells Berroco, Cascade, Debbie Bliss, DMC, Hoooked, King Cole, Lion Brand, Nako, Rico, Sirdar

Michaels
Online sales and store locator
www.michaels.com
Sells Caron, DMC, Hoooked, Lion Brand

WEBS
Online sales and store
www.yarn.com
Sells Berroco, Cascade Yarns, Debbie Bliss, DMC, Katia, Rico, Sirdar

AUSTRALIA

Prestige Yarns
Online sales and stockist locator
www.prestigeyarns.com.au

Sun Spun
Online sales and store
www.sunspun.com.au
Sells Cascade, Sirdar

TexYarns
Online sales and stockist locator
www.texyarns.com
Sells Katia

YARN BRANDS

Bergere de France
www.bergeredefrance.co.uk (UK)
www.bergeredefrance.com (US)

Berroco
www.berroco.com

Caron
www.caron-yarn.com

Cascade
www.cascadeyarns.com

Debbie Bliss
www.debbieblissonline.com

DMC
www.dmc.com

Hoooked
www.hoookedyarn.com

Katia
www.katia.com

King Cole
www.kingcole.com

Lion Brand
www.lionbrand.com

Madelinetosh
www.madelinetosh.com

Rico
www.rico-design.de/en

Sirdar
www.sirdar.com

WelcomeYarn
www.welcomeyarn.pt

index

acknowledgements

First I have to thank Rachel Atkinson for her relentless, infinite patience when tackling my pattern writing, she is phenomenal. Thanks also to Penny Craig and the crew at CICO Books for their patience and understanding when dealing with my 'creative process' – they help me grow all of the time! A massive thank you to Jenni at LoveCrochet for all of the encouragement, support and extremely prompt deliveries, as well as Cara at DMC for some beautiful yarns, and last but by no means least, Jemima Bicknell for her meticulous pattern checking.

And as ever, I thank my very special family for all their continual inspiration and support.